One Thing Needful:

An Invitation to the Study of Worship

Revised and Updated

By

Gary M. Mathena, DMin

WESTBOW®
P R E S S
A DIVISION OF THOMAS NELSON
& ZONDERVAN

NIV – New International Version
Scripture taken from the Holy Bible, New International Version®. Copyright © 1973,
1978, 1984 Biblica. Used by permission of Zondervan. All rights reserved.

ESV – English Standard Version
Scripture quotations are from The Holy Bible, English Standard Version® (ESV®), copyright © 2001 by
Crossway, a publishing ministry of Good News Publishers. Used by permission. All rights reserved.

NKJV – New King James Version
Scripture taken from the New King James Version. Copyright 1979, 1980, 1982
by Thomas Nelson, inc. Used by permission. All rights reserved.

Cover image: Jesus, Mary, and Martha by Anton Dorph. Used by permission
of the Hope Gallery and Museum of Fine Art, Salt Lake City, Utah.

WestBow Press books may be ordered through booksellers or by contacting:

WestBow Press
A Division of Thomas Nelson & Zondervan
1663 Liberty Drive
Bloomington, IN 47403
www.westbowpress.com
1 (866) 928-1240

Because of the dynamic nature of the Internet, any web addresses or links contained in
this book may have changed since publication and may no longer be valid. The views
expressed in this work are solely those of the author and do not necessarily reflect the
views of the publisher, and the publisher hereby disclaims any responsibility for them.

Any people depicted in stock imagery provided by Thinkstock are models,
and such images are being used for illustrative purposes only.
Certain stock imagery © Thinkstock.

ISBN: 978-1-4908-8961-0 (sc)
ISBN: 978-1-4908-8963-4 (hc)
ISBN: 978-1-4908-8962-7 (e)

Library of Congress Control Number: 2015913950

Print information available on the last page.

WestBow Press rev. date: 02/04/2016

To Donnita

God is trying to call us back to that for which He created us—
to worship Him and to enjoy Him forever!

—A. W. Tozer, *Whatever Happened To Worship?*

Contents

Foreword

I have known and been a friend of Gary Mathena for many years. But I never truly appreciated the man until both Gary and I spent a week teaching in the Worship Studies program at Liberty University a few years back. In addition to Gary and me, there were several other teachers of varying stages of renown. It was a bracing week for all of us.

What I observed then was that God used Gary in a unique and powerful way to communicate biblical truth. I noticed that his teachings were packed with more useful content than the rest of ours put together. Since that week, I have been a full-on Gary Mathena fan. I can't tell you what an honor it is for me to fully endorse his wonderful book.

Just another book on worship? Not by any means! *One Thing Needful* does perhaps the most *needful* thing a worship book can do—it goes straight to the heart of what worship is, and why and how God wants us to practice it, undergirded with all the biblical support I have come to expect from this rock-solid man of God.

I have learned much from reading this book. There are a few things I will never understand—or teach—in the same way again. For instance, have you ever considered the subtlety of what it means to be created in the very image of God? Chapter 2. Or three significant things man lost by sinning in the Garden of Eden? Chapter 5. How about the many ways Jesus specifically fulfills each facet of the design of the Hebrew tabernacle? Also Chapter 5. And, for that matter, have you seen the ways Jesus is personified through every book of the Bible? Chapter 6. I could fill up pages and pages of nuggets like this that work together to build on Gary's great theme—truly the greatest theme.

Somehow, Gary manages to share deep truths like these with a writing style that captures his personality without our wanting to bolt for the exits to escape some boring lecture. I know Gary as a man who loves both God and people, and he communicates in a way that captivates.

If you are one who values learning God's designs and the great Heart behind them, you must read *One Thing Needful*. It is a living, breathing examination of the single most important assignment in all of creation, and it can literally change your life.

—Dave Williamson, Author, *God's Singers*

Preface

*I say that the greatest tragedy in the world today is
that God has made man in his image and made him
to worship him, made him to play the harp of worship
before the face of God day and night, but he has failed
God and dropped the harp. It lies voiceless at his feet.*

—A. W. Tozer

It has been my delight to be a minister of music for over forty-five years in churches with memberships of less than a hundred to congregations numbering many thousands. I have had the opportunity to lead worship in practically every possible setting, ranging from sitting under a tree with a group of schoolchildren in Zimbabwe; to playing my trumpet on a crowded street corner in San Salvador; to standing under the Superdome in New Orleans leading tens of thousands in congregational praise. Within the context of my calling as an ordained minister of the gospel in worship leadership, I have, over the years, been a student of the fascinating doctrine of worship both informally and formally.

Not too many years ago, I was asked by Dr. Charles Williams, president of Southern Baptist School for Biblical Studies in Jacksonville, Florida, to design a program of study for the school by which a student could major in worship at the bachelor's, master's and doctoral degree levels. This book is a distillation of that research and is presented in this form for the purpose of inspiring others to gain a thorough understanding of exactly what it means to worship God. This book is designed not only for the pastor, minister of music, and worship leader, but also and especially for the layman who is interested in learning more about Christian worship and is looking for some direction on what should be studied and how to go about it.

The seed thought for this project was an article I read by the late Dr. Robert E. Webber, then professor of theology at Wheaton College and recognized authority on Christian worship, entitled "Preparations for Becoming a Worship Leader." In this article, Dr. James White, professor of liturgy at Notre Dame, in a conversation with Webber, observed that most people think that a study of worship is fundamentally a music issue and has to do with the leading and planning of actual worship services. While that is certainly one facet of worship study, it is much more than that. Webber pointed out that preparing for worship leadership "is more comprehensive in nature and scope than anything else in ministry."[1]

A student and leader of worship should study worship in the Old Testament, especially tabernacle worship, the sacrificial system, the feasts and festivals, and the idea of covenant. Old Testament worship, with its types and symbols, sets the stage for a study of New Testament worship, in which the church makes the transition from temple and synagogue worship to worship that is distinctively Christian.

A worship leader needs to understand the historical roots of our present worship practices. Our worship today has been built upon over twenty centuries of worship heritage: the early church, the medieval church, the Reformation era, modern Protestant worship, and the many contemporary worship cultures. It is important to know why we worship as we do. We cannot know who we *are* as a worshipping community until we understand who we *were*.

Jesus says in John 4:24, "God is Spirit: and those who worship Him must worship in spirit and truth." Jesus defines "truth" in John 17:17 as He intercedes on behalf of His disciples, "Sanctify them by Your truth. Your word is truth." Worship must be based on Scripture. As we need to be biblical in our worship, the Word of God is our ultimate worship manual. Therefore, we need to study the theology of worship.

A worship leader needs an understanding of the role of music and the arts in worship from a biblical and historical point of view. He should appreciate the relationship between worship and the other ministries of the church. He needs to know how to plan and lead a worship service. Most importantly, a worship leader needs to be a worshipper himself. A guide cannot lead where he has not been. A worship leader, if he is to be effective, must have a lifestyle of worship.

Based upon this philosophy, in the chapters that follow, seven worship study disciplines will be introduced, along with further reading recommendations listed for each chapter at the end of the book. These seven worship study disciplines are Introduction to Worship, Theology of Worship, History of Worship, Tabernacle Worship, Music and Worship, The Heart of the Worship Leader, and Lifestyle Worship. The treatment given these seven worship disciplines here should by no means be considered exhaustive studies of these topics, but rather should be considered as spiritual appetizers to whet the reader's appetite for more extensive study in the suggested texts.

May God's blessing be upon this endeavor, and may this work be used by the Holy Spirit to teach men and women the indescribable joy of worshipping our wonderful Lord.

Let the words of my mouth and the
meditation of my heart
Be acceptable in Your sight,
O LORD, my strength, and my Redeemer.
Psalm 19:14

Acknowledgements

I would like to express my appreciation to all the wonderful churches where I have had the privilege to serve over the last forty-five years of music ministry: Twin Oaks Baptist Church, Oklahoma City, Oklahoma; Canadian Heights Baptist Church, Yukon, Oklahoma; Windsor Hills Baptist Church, Oklahoma City; County Line Baptist Church, Oklahoma City; First Southern Baptist Church, Del City, Oklahoma; Valley Baptist Church, Bakersfield, California; and First Baptist Church, Roanoke, Virginia. I am so thankful for each precious congregation for their love, prayers, and support and for the opportunity to learn from them and to lead them in this most holy calling as a worship leader.

Thanks to Malinda Harris (now in heaven) and Marilyn Whygle who helped me with the preparation of the original manuscript. A special word of appreciation goes to my friend, Drew Gibbons, for her most excellent editing skills in preparation for this updated and revised edition. I would like to thank my mother and father, Dr. Harold and Patricia Mathena, who were used by God to instill in me a desire to worship Him and serve Him with my life, and who have encouraged me in this endeavor with their myriad affirmations and constant prayers.

I would like to especially express my gratitude to Dr. Charles Williams of Southern Baptist School for Biblical Studies in Jacksonville, Florida, for his friendship and guidance in this project.

My eternal love and gratitude goes to Donnita, Leah, and Rebecca—my precious family—without whose patience, understanding, and encouragement, none of this would have been possible.

Chapter 1

One Thing Needful

And she had a sister called Mary, which also
sat at Jesus' feet and heard His word.

—Luke 10:39

She was busy in the kitchen, as she always was, when there came a knock at the door. She wasn't expecting any visitors and was a little aggravated at the thought of an uninvited guest spoiling her plans for the afternoon. As she approached the door, wiping her hands with her apron, she was heard muttering something about there not being enough hours in the day. Imagine her surprise as she swung open the door to find the Lord Jesus and twelve hungry disciples standing there. Of course, she immediately asked them in, and after making them comfortable and apologizing for the house being in a mess, Martha went into action.

Martha had quite a reputation as being the best cook in all of Bethany. Nobody could set a table like her. When she was in her kitchen, she was in her element. She whizzed and flitted around with authority and skill, assembling ingredients, heating the oil, pouring the water, and fixing the fruit plate just so. She was determined to fix a meal for Christ that He would not soon forget. After all, she had a reputation to maintain.

In her preparation for this great meal, we see something *commendable*. She so loved Jesus that she wanted this meal to be her very best. She wanted to honor Him in its serving. But at the same time, we also see something *condemnable*. I'm not sure when it happened, but at some point, Martha's ministry *for* Christ began to take priority over her

1

relationship *with* Christ. Sadly, that is not an uncommon occurrence in the life of a believer. It is a very subtle shift that can go almost undetected if we aren't careful to recognize the signs. How do we know when we are about to cross that fine line? The Scripture teaches us in Galatians 6:9 that we should not become "weary while doing good." With every task that God requires of us, He always enables us to perform it. Finding ourselves overwhelmed and anxious in our ministry for Christ is a sure sign that we have stepped beyond God's requirement and, subsequently, the enabling to accomplish it.

The Holy Spirit is the fuel that energizes us for service; our body—our heart, soul, mind, and strength—is the wick. When we are operating in the power of the Holy Spirit, we are burning oil; our wick is sustained, and our lamp burns bright and clear. When our lamp is drained because of spiritual business and misplaced priorities, however, we begin to burn the wick and we are soon used up. Consequently, we tend to put out a lot of smoke as well.

My dad used to tell us that one of his chores as a boy was to tend to the kerosene lamps that were used in his home. If they had not been trimmed properly or if he had let them run out of oil, they would begin to smoke and cloud the chimney. From that time forward, when any of us would get a little irritable and out of sorts in our home, someone would point out the fact that our "chimney was getting a little cloudy."

There is the sin of not doing enough, but there is also the sin of doing more than enough. Moses needed only to speak to the rock; instead, he went too far and struck it. Saul should have killed all the sheep and oxen as God had commanded; instead, he went too far and kept the best to sacrifice to God. God reminded Saul through Samuel that "to obey is better than sacrifice" (1 Samuel 15:22).

Not only do we see something *commendable* and something *condemnable* in this story, but at least from Martha's point of view, we can also see something *contemptible*. Martha could not believe that Mary could be so thoughtless as to leave her with all the meal preparations. Martha, busy "serving Christ," thinks she has grounds to be angry with her "lazy" sister, and even chides Jesus for allowing the injustice to continue. Her contempt for Mary's choice to sit at Jesus' feet manifested her lack of spirituality. She was one of those whom Paul wrote about in Philippians

3:19 who had "set their mind on earthly things". In all of her religious activity, she had completely overlooked the spiritual activity going on around her. How surprised she must have been when Jesus sweetly and lovingly rebuked her, "Martha, Martha, you are worried and troubled about many things" (Luke 10:42).

As many as Christ loves, He chastens, and He certainly loved Martha. He told her that all the fussing and fretting over making the meal was commendable, but there was really only one thing needful, and that was to sit at His feet and learn of Him. All the meetings and classes we attend, all the Christian work we do, all the organizations we administer, and all the other things we do in service to Christ are good and fine, but we must constantly remind ourselves that there is only one thing needful, and that is to commune with Him in adoration and worship. We must be careful that we don't cross that fine line where our ministry *for* Christ becomes more important to us that our relationship *with* Christ. It's amazing to me how easy it is to neglect Him while we are so busy doing things for Him.

In Luke's account of the boy Jesus at the temple, it is interesting to note that Jesus was *lost to the strangest people—His very own*. When I was teaching this chapter at the Bethlehem Bible College in the Holy Land not long ago, one dear lady took exception to the idea that Jesus was "lost." I think the misunderstanding was probably the result of my interpreter giving a very literal interpretation of my comments. So, in the interest of clarity, let me say that I do not believe that Jesus Himself was lost—He knew exactly where He was and what He was doing, but He was lost to Mary and Joseph. He was lost to the ones who loved Him the most. I have always marveled at John 1:11 that says, "He came to his own, and his own did not receive Him."

Jesus was *lost in the strangest place—the House of God*. Jesus has become lost in the midst of all our religious activity and ecclesiastical efficiency. Like the Ephesian church in Revelation 2:4, we have left our first love. Jesus, standing outside His church, pleads with us, "Behold, I stand at the door, and knock. If anyone hears My voice and opens the door, I will come in to him, and dine with him, and he with Me" (Revelation 3:20).

Not only was Jesus lost to the strangest people and in the strangest place, but He was also *lost in the strangest way—simply by neglect*. Jesus' parents *"supposing* Him to have been in the company ... went a day's journey" (Luke 2:44, emphasis added). How many times have we, in the excitement and chaos of the moment, gone a day's journey only to discover that we have left Jesus behind? Like Joseph and Mary, we become frantic and confused and simply have to go back to the place where we left Him. We who serve Christ vocationally in the local church stand in the greatest danger of losing Him in all the hectic hurry-scurry of ministry. Jesus was lost to the strangest people—His very own; He was lost in the strangest place—the House of God; and He was lost in the strangest way—simply by neglect.

My prayer is that in these pages you will hear His gentle knock, and His still, small voice, inviting you to turn aside from your clamoring calendar and your insistent itinerary, to commune with Him and to worship at His feet. After all, there is really only one thing needful.

Chapter 2

Worship's Purpose: Introduction to Worship

I know of no pleasure so rich, none so pure,
none so hallowing in their influences, and
constant in their supply, as those which result
from the true and spiritual worship of God.

—Richard Watson

There is a mind-set in some evangelical circles today that worship is just another spoke on the wheel of the church program along with the preaching program, the music program, the education program, the evangelism program, the missions program, and so on. My contention is that worship is not just *a* program of the church, but rather it is *the* program of the church. It is not just another spoke on the wheel, but the very hub from which everything else should emanate. In this chapter that introduces you to the study of worship, consider with me these three important truths: we have been *created* to worship, we have been *commanded* to worship, and we have been *called* to worship.

We Have Been Created to Worship

Isaiah 43:7 teaches us that we were created for the purpose of worshipping God and giving Him glory, "Everyone who is called by My name, whom I have created for My glory," as does Revelation 4:11, "You are worthy, O

Lord, to receive glory and honor and power; for you created all things, and by Your will they exist and were created." *Worship is our design.*

Ezra records for us in 2 Chronicles 5-7 what was probably the greatest worship service in all of history when Solomon dedicated the magnificent temple that he had just completed. He tells us that

> It was the *duty* of the trumpeters and singers to make themselves heard in unison in praise and thanksgiving to the LORD, and when the song was raised, with trumpets and cymbals and other musical instruments, in praise to the LORD, "For he is good, for his steadfast love endures forever," the house, the house of the LORD, was filled with a cloud. (2 Chronicles 5:13 ESV, emphasis added)

The trumpeters and singers were duty-bound "to make themselves heard" as they offered praise and thanksgiving to God in their worship.

The Apostle Paul uses the beautiful imagery of temple worship as he describes for us the work of his ministry in the following:

> I have written you quite boldly on some points, as if to remind you of them again, because of the grace God gave me to be a minister of Christ Jesus to the Gentiles with the priestly *duty* of proclaiming the gospel of God, so that the Gentiles might become an offering acceptable to God, sanctified by the Holy Spirit. Therefore I glory in Christ Jesus in my service to God. (Romans 15:15-17 NIV, emphasis added)

Paul considered the proclamation of the gospel his priestly duty and an act of worship as he glorified Christ Jesus in his service to God.

Solomon, the wisest man who ever lived, after having investigated thoroughly the pursuit of happiness and the meaning of life wrote, "Let us hear the conclusion of the whole matter: Fear God, and keep his commandments: for this is the whole duty of man" (Ecclesiastes 12:13 KJV). *Worship is our duty.*

God, in describing the kind of worship that pleases Him, said, "Yet they seek me daily, and *delight* to know My ways … they take *delight* in approaching God" (Isaiah 58:2, emphasis added). And the apostle Paul wrote, "For to me, to live is Christ" (Philippians 1:21). In other words, Paul's very reason for living—his ultimate *delight*—was to worship Christ and glorify Him with his life. *Worship is our delight.*

In fact, the purpose for all of creation is the glory of God, as follows:

> The heavens were created for God's glory (Psalm 19:1). The earth was created for God's glory (Isaiah 6:3). The seas were created for God's glory (Psalm 98:7).
>
> Christ's birth was for God's glory (Luke 2:14). Christ's life was for God's glory (John 17:4). Christ's death was for God's glory (John 13:31-32).
>
> Praise is for God's glory (Psalm 50:23). Prayer is for God's glory (John 14:13). Preaching is for God's glory (Galatians 1:11-24).
>
> Suffering is for God's glory (1 Peter 4:16). Salvation is for God's glory (Exodus 14:13-18). Soul winning is for God's glory (Matthew 28:19).
>
> Childhood is for God's glory (Mathew 21:16). Youth is for God's glory (1 Timothy 4:12). Old age is for God's glory (Psalm 71:18).
>
> Our bodies are for God's glory (1 Corinthians 6:20). Our sickness is for God's glory (John 11:4). Our healing is for God's glory (Matthew 15:29-31).
>
> Our works are for God's glory (Matthew 5:16). Our words are for God's glory (1 Peter 4:11). Our worship is for God's glory (1 Chronicles 16:28-29).
>
> Life is for God's glory (Philippians 1:21). Death is for the glory of God (John 21:19). And the apostle Paul sums it all up when he said, "Therefore, whether you eat or drink, or whatever you do, do all to the glory of God" (1 Corinthians 10:31).

The fact that we were created to worship God and to reflect His glory to the world is demonstrated throughout the biblical record.

The Example of Adam and Eve

Moses wrote in Genesis 1:26 and 27, "Then God said, 'Let us make man in Our image, according to Our likeness … ' So God created man in His own image; in the image of God He created him." The word "image" is translated from the Hebrew word *tselem*, which means "likeness, resemblance, and a representative figure." Used five times in the Old Testament to refer to man as being created in the image of God, Spiros Zodhiates, commenting on this word, wrote, "God made man in such a way as to reflect some of His own perfections—perfect in knowledge, righteousness, and holiness, with dominion over the creatures (Genesis 1:26)."[1] We were designed to reflect God's glory—to be His representatives upon the earth!

Some theologians believe that Adam and Eve, in their innocent state, were actually "clothed" with the reflected *Shekinah* of the Almighty. Following is how one writer eloquently described it:

> Never had bridal pair so beautiful and radiant apparel. The unclothed bodies of our first parents we can imagine were enswathed in ethereal and transfiguring light; in their case the outshining of their holy souls, which, as yet, were the undimmed and unmarred image of their Maker, capable of receiving and reflecting his glory.[2]

Perhaps the reason why, before their disobedience, Adam and Eve were unaware of their nakedness was because they were clothed in the reflected glory of God. Perhaps some quality is designed into the very molecular structure of our skin that absorbs and reflects the glory of God as we abide in His presence with a pure and holy heart. Romans 3:23 says, "For all have sinned and fall short of the glory of God." When Adam and Eve sinned, they came short of God's glory—they no longer represented the character of God or reflected God's purity and holiness—and as a result, their lights went out. For the first time, they saw one another disrobed of the righteousness and glory of God, and they were ashamed.

The Example of Moses

Remember in Exodus 34 that Moses, after having come from that wonderful worship experience in the presence of God on Sinai, "did not know that the skin of his face shone while he talked with Him" (Exodus 34:29). There was something about that worship experience that energized the molecules of Moses' face in such a way as to cause his countenance to glow, reflecting God's glory, and affirming to everyone that he had been in the presence of God.

The Example of Jesus

Matthew wrote how that Jesus took Peter, James, and John up on a high mountain where Jesus "was transfigured before them. His face shone like the sun, and his clothes became as white as the light" (Matthew 17:1-2). The first Adam lost the ability to reflect the glory of God because of sin; the Second Adam, the Lord Jesus, who knew no sin, radiated the glory of God. The writer of Hebrews in describing Christ said that He is "the brightness of [God's] glory and the express image of His person" (Hebrews 1:3). Here the two thoughts of brightness and image are brought together again in the person of the Second Adam. The word translated "transfigured" in Matthew 17 is the Greek word *metamorphoo*, the same word used in Romans 12:2 translated "transformed" in the KJV.[3] We get our word *metamorphosis* from this word, which suggests allowing what is on the inside to show on the outside. For that brief moment, God allowed the disciples to witness the reflected glory of God tabernacled in Christ. What was on the inside was seen on the outside. Paul writes,

> But even if our gospel is veiled, it is veiled to those who are perishing, whose minds the god of this age has blinded, who do not believe, lest the light of the gospel of the glory of Christ, who is the image of God, should shine on them … For it is the God who commanded light to shine out of darkness, who has shone in our hearts to give the light of the knowledge of the glory of God in the face of Jesus Christ. (2 Corinthians 4:3-4,6)

Notice that Paul refers to Christ in the same words that Moses referred to Adam; they both are "the image of God." The Greek word *eikon* translated "image," means "to be like, to resemble," which "always assumes a prototype, that which it not merely resembles, but from which it is drawn. Thus, the reflection of the sun on the water is *eikon*."[4] The reflection cannot exist without the sun—it draws its very essence from its source. As the water reflects the brilliant sunlight, so God's glory was reflected "in the face of Jesus Christ" just as it was reflected in the face of Moses. The word *veiled* reminds us of Moses' veil that covered his shining countenance.

The Example of Stephen

Stephen, one of the first deacons of the early church, was being used mightily by the Holy Spirit. The Scripture says that Stephen was "full of faith and power, [and] did great wonders and signs among the people" (Acts 6:8).

There were those in the synagogue who rose up against Stephen, accusing him of speaking against Moses and God. As Stephen stood before his accusers, the Bible says that, "all who sat in the council, looking steadfastly at him, saw his face as the face of an angel" (Acts 6:15). What is the identifying quality of an angelic face? Matthew describes the angel's face at Jesus' empty tomb. "His countenance was like lightning, and his clothing as white as snow" (Matthew 28:3). And John tells us in Revelation 10:1, "I saw still another mighty angel coming down from heaven, clothed with a cloud. And a rainbow was on his head, his face was like the sun." To have the face of an angel then is to have a face that illuminates like lightning and shines like the sun.

God validated the ministry of Stephen so appropriately before his accusers by allowing his face to actually shine, as Moses' face did, after having been in God's presence.

The Example of Our Own Glorified Bodies

Not only did Adam, Moses, Jesus, and Stephen reflect the glory of God in their physical countenance, but the Bible says that there will come a day when we also will receive our glorified bodies and "then the righteous will shine forth as the sun in the kingdom of their Father" (Matthew 13:43). Our earthly bodies are the temples of the Holy Spirit of God—we actually house God's manifest presence, the *Shekinah*. Perhaps the only thing keeping what is on the inside from showing and glowing on the outside is our veiled bodies, stained with sin.

When Christ returns, these earthy bodies will be done away with, and we will be changed—transformed—and we will receive our new incorruptible bodies, like Adam had before the Fall, and like Christ had after His resurrection—bodies with the ability to absorb and reflect the glory of God. As Christ's garments glowed there on the Mount of Transfiguration, there will come a glorious day when we, too, shall shine in our glorified bodies. The veil of our bodies will be taken away, and what has been hidden in the secret place of personal holiness before God, hidden in Christ, will burst forth in radiant glory. "He shall bring forth your righteousness as the light, and your justice as the noonday" (Psalm 37:6). We will once again be totally and completely the *eikon*—the "image"—the reflection—of God Almighty.

Did God actually create our skin with the ability to physically glow in His presence? I think a good argument could be made that He did. In any case, the point of this whole line of thought is to emphasize that we were indeed created to manifest God's glory, and as we live our lives in such a way as to represent Him on this earth—reflecting His glory—we are engaged in vital spiritual worship.

We Have Been Commanded to Worship

Not only have we been created to worship, but also we have been *commanded* to worship. When asked by one of the scribes which of all the commandments was the greatest, Jesus replied, "'You shall love the LORD your God with all your heart, with all your soul, with all your mind, and with all your strength.' This is the first commandment" (Mark 12:30). The Greek word *agapao*, translated "love," is a word that is used to refer to our love for God and God's love toward us and infers finding one's joy in something or someone.[5] This type of love can easily be equated with worship, for one of the actual dictionary definitions of worship is "extravagant respect or admiration for or devotion to an object of esteem."[6] This is exactly the kind of love Jesus is talking about in Mark 12:30. Christ calls us to show extravagant devotion to God—to find our joy in Him and Him alone—and to worship God with every fiber of our beings: with our hearts (our wills and desires), with our souls (our emotions and affections), with our minds (our intellects and understanding), and with our strength (our skills and abilities).[7] Paul begged us to present our bodies as "a living sacrifice, holy, acceptable to God" (Romans 12:1-2). The Hebrew worshipper would not have even considered offering God a partial sacrifice. Our devotion must be whole if it is to be holy.

John the Evangelist gives us five specific ways we can actually know if we have this whole-hearted love for God.

> (1) *We will be obedient to His Word.* "But whoever keeps His word, truly the love of God is perfected in him." (1 John 2:5)

> (2) *We will not love the world.* "Do not love the world or the things in the world. If anyone loves the world, the love of the Father is not in him." (1 John 2:15)

> (3) *We will provide for the needs of others.* "But whoever has this world's goods, and sees his brother in need, and shuts up his

heart from him, how does the love of God abide in him?" (1 John 3:17)

(4) *We will love one another.* "Beloved, let us love one another, for love is of God; and everyone that loves is born of God, and knows God." (1 John 4:7)

(5) *We will not hate anyone.* "If someone says, 'I love God,' and hates his brother, he is a liar; for he who does not love his brother whom he has seen, how can he love God whom he has not seen? And this commandment we have from him: that he who loves God must love his brother also." (1 John 4:20)

Loving God with a whole heart is not just some nebulous nuance of emotion; it is evidenced in the actions of our heart, soul, mind, and strength. That's why Jesus said in Mark 12:31 that the second most important commandment was like the first, in that we should love our neighbor as our selves. Our love for God will be confirmed by our actions, especially as they relate to others. As Robert Webber noted in the title of his book, *Worship Is a Verb.*[8] Worship is love in action. Since the first and greatest commandment is to love God with all our heart, soul, mind, and strength, our failure to do so on a daily basis would be the first and greatest sin we could commit. Man's greatest failure is his failure to worship God exclusively and completely.

We Have Been Called to Worship

We have been *created* to worship, we have been *commanded* to worship, and we have been *called* to worship. Ben Patterson in his book *The Grand Essentials* says that we as the church of God may have many occupations, but only one vocation. The Latin word *vocare,* from which we get our English word *vocation,* means "to call." Our vocation is our calling. The Greek word used in Scripture for "a calling," is *klesis.* We see it in the Greek word for "church," *ekklesia*—the called out. The church has been called out vocationally to worship God.[9] First Peter 2:9 says, "But you are a chosen generation, a royal priesthood, a holy nation, His own special people, that you may proclaim the praises of Him who called you out of darkness into His marvelous light."

A fire chief was training some new recruits, barking orders and making assignments. He assigned one man to polish the bell, another to tend the hoses, another to wash the truck, and another to cook. He continued until all the jobs were filled. After he made the assignments, he went back to the first man in line and asked, "Now, what's your job?" The young rookie timidly replied, "To polish the bell, sir." Upon hearing that the chief put his nose against the nose of that young fireman and shouted, "No! That is not your job! Your job is putting out fires!"

The point was well made. There are many necessary duties that must be attended to in the course of our ministry—many occupations that occupy our time—but we must never allow our occupations to take precedence over the vocation to which we have been called—the worship of God.

We have been *created* to worship. We have been *commanded* to worship. We have been *called* to worship. The study of Christian worship is critical, therefore, because it is the essence of all we are in Christ and all we do for His glory.

Chapter 3

Worship's Procedure: Theology of Worship

Perhaps the greatest need in all of Christendom
is for a clear understanding of the biblical
teaching about worship. When the church fails to
worship properly, it fails in every other area. And
the world is suffering because of its failure.

—John MacArthur

Many years ago, an Egyptian farmer decided he wanted to build a farm out in the desert. As he was making plans to build his house, he searched for just the right spot and dug in different areas until he found what he thought was a solid stone foundation upon which to build. Over time, the sand began to shift away from the house, revealing more of the flat stone foundation upon which the farmer had built. He then noticed for the first time that chiseled on the flat surface of the rock were intricate carvings and surmised that he had built his house on some ancient fallen column. As the archeologists began to dig around the stone, they discovered that the column was not lying down at all but was still standing up! Deeper and deeper they dug until finally, after the excavation was completed, the farmer's house stood atop a stone column 80 feet in the air![1]

This Egyptian farmer knew nothing of the foundation upon which he had built his home. In much the same way, many Christians today know very little, if anything, of the tremendous breadth and depth of the biblical foundations upon which their worship theology and practices are built. Most Christians have a very shallow understanding of what worship is really all about, and as a result, there is much confusion and misunderstanding as to what accounts for genuine biblical worship.

What follows are three important principles that will help and guide you in formulating your own theology of worship. First of all, notice with me that …

A Right Theology of Worship Is Balanced

A right theology of Christian worship is absolutely critical to the success of a Christian's walk with God. "Christian" worship must be founded upon biblical principles, or it is not Christian at all. Jesus said to the woman of Samaria,

> But the hour is coming, and now is, when the true worshippers will worship the Father in spirit and truth; for the Father is seeking such to worship him. God is Spirit, and those who worship Him must worship in spirit and truth. (John 4:23-24)

In these two verses we see both the subjective ("in spirit") and the objective ("in truth") sides of worship. Warren Wiersbe emphasized the "in truth" side of worship when he wrote, "If we do not submit to some kind of objective revelation, some Word from God, then our worship is ignorant and probably false."[2] At the same time, we need to understand that worship devoid of "spirit" (emotion and personal experience) is empty, dull, and lifeless. A "spiritless" worshipper is in danger of becoming like those the apostle Paul warned Timothy about in 2 Timothy 3:5, those "having a form of godliness but denying its power."

When it comes to a right theology of worship, a proper balance between spirit and truth is vitally important. If we are out of balance in Christendom at large today between spirit and truth, it is because we are heavy on spirit and light on truth. We tend to be more concerned with our own personal worship experiences than with whether or not those experiences are biblical and pleasing to God.

One subtle example of this can be seen in some circles of the present church growth movement. There is a dangerous mind-set that advocates *using* worship as a means to the end of attracting people to our churches.

We have lost sight of the fact that worship is not designed so that we might please ourselves, but that we might please God. He should be the focus of our attention when we think about worship, not our own self-gratification. This is illustrated best when we make comments like, "I didn't get anything out of worship today," or, "I didn't like the songs today," or, "I'm not having my needs met," or something else along those lines. The person who makes comments like these is not engaged in God-worship, but in self-worship. The focal point of their thinking is not "Was God pleased?" but rather "Was I pleased?"

The biblical worshipper never comes to a worship service to receive, but to give. From the very beginning, worship has always been about the offering—the sacrifice given to God. There has been a lot of talk over the last few years about the "worship wars," as if disagreement over worship styles was something new. Actually, the very first worship war was recorded in Genesis 4. There was a disagreement between Cain and his brother, Abel, about what constitutes appropriate worship, and the controversy had to do with the offering. Cain was a farmer, so he brought to worship an offering of produce from his crops. Abel was a shepherd, so he brought "the best portions of the firstborn lambs from his flock" (Genesis 4:4 NLT). God accepted Abel's offering, but rejected Cain's, as it does matter to God how we approach Him in worship. In a fit of anger and jealousy, Cain killed his brother. The first murder in history was the result of the "worship wars," and it all had to do with the offering.

There is no worship without an offering. The whole sacrificial system laid out by Moses was about the offering. Tabernacle and temple worship was all about the offering. The reason the biblical worshipper came to worship was not to sing songs, or hear a sermon, or even to receive a blessing. It was to bring the offering. The biblical worshipper would not have dared come to the altar empty-handed.

Think for a moment about the last time you went to church. Now, let me ask you a question, "Did you have a genuine worship experience?" You may say, "Well, I was really touched by the songs we sang. I was actually moved to tears." Or you may say something like, "Well, I really got a lot out of the message. It really spoke to the need of my heart." Now all of those things are good, and things like that can and do happen in the context of worship, but those things in and of themselves are not genuine worship.

The test of whether genuine worship has taken place is not in asking, "Did I *get* anything?" but instead "Did I *give* anything?" Worship is not about what God gives you, but rather what you give God. I would dare say that 99 percent of us who go to worship on any given Sunday have spent absolutely no time at all thinking about the offering we are bringing to God. We come to worship empty-handed, totally consumed with thoughts of what we are going to get out of it, instead of thinking and praying about what we are bringing to it.

To be clear, when I speak of the offering we are bringing to God, I'm not speaking, necessarily, about the money we may put in the offering plate when it comes by, but rather the offering of our bodies—our hearts, souls, minds, and strengths—given as living sacrifices to God (Romans 12:1).

When it comes to worship, it *is* better to give than to receive, because it is in the act of bringing our offering to God with no agenda or ulterior motive that we receive our highest fulfillment as a creature created for worship. A person with the agenda of receiving a blessing from worship will always go away disappointed because worship was not designed necessarily to be a blessing to us. Remember, worship is not about *you*— it's always about God. "Bless *the LORD,* O my soul; and all that is within me, bless *His* holy name!" (Psalm 103:1, emphasis added). Paradoxically, a person who comes to worship, not for their own personal benefit, but for the express purpose of being a blessing to God, will always go away blessed with a great sense of fulfillment and joy, because we were not created for our pleasure but for His. "Thou art worthy, O Lord to receive glory and honor and power: for thou hast created all things, and for *thy* pleasure they are and were created" (Revelation 4:11 KJV, emphasis added).

It is important to understand that for real worship to take place, it cannot be a means to an end, but rather must be an end in itself. The purpose of worship can be nothing less than Godward veneration, or it is at best idolatry of self. I'm afraid that most of what we call worship in our churches today has more to do with us and our personal preferences than it has to do with God and what pleases Him. A. W. Tozer wrote, "Worship is no longer worship when it reflects the culture around us more than the Christ within us."[3] A right theology of worship will help us to maintain this important balance between spirit and truth.

A Right Theology of Worship Is Basic

The basic importance of a right worship theology in understanding the ultimate purpose for our redemption can be seen historically as we realize that the first two sins recorded in the Bible were related to this very issue. Moses recounts the tragic story, "So when the woman saw that the tree was good for food, that it was pleasant to the eyes, and a tree desirable to make one wise, she took of its fruit and ate. She also gave to her husband with her, and he ate" (Genesis 3:6).

Adam and Eve decided that it was more important that their worship please themselves than please God, and as a result "sin entered the world, and death through sin, and thus death spread to all men" (Romans 5:12). How ironic that "a tree desirable to make one wise" actually revealed their ignorance of the importance of a right theology of worship. The tragedy did not stop there, but was played out in the lives of Adam's children years later.

A moment ago, we talked about Cain and Abel and the first worship war recorded in the Bible. Why was it that God rejected Cain's offering of the fruits and vegetables that he had raised, but accepted Abel's offering of the very best of the firstborn lambs? God had set the precedent with Adam and Eve at the incident of the Tree of Knowledge of Good and Evil that sin could only be atoned for and their nakedness covered by the slaying of an innocent victim. Human good, represented by the fig leaves with which they tried to cover themselves, is never adequate. Blood had to be shed to acquire the skins to cover their nakedness. Later, that principle would be codified in the Old Covenant and fulfilled in the New that without the shedding of blood there can be no covering, or forgiveness, of sin (Hebrews 9:22). In his pride, Cain, like his parents, chose to ignore the basic importance of a right theology of worship and suffered the consequences in envy, anger, murder, and banishment.

An understanding of the concept of redemption is basic to an understanding of a biblical theology of worship. In fact, we are redeemed that we *might* worship. Most Christians believe they have been saved so they might escape hell and gain heaven. Although, that is certainly a wonderful benefit of salvation, it is not the primary reason for it. Ultimately, our redemption is not about us. It is never all about us. It is always all about God. Our redemption is about God reclaiming and restoring us to our created purpose as worshippers before His throne in resolution of the angelic conflict. We'll talk more about the angelic conflict in the chapter on lifestyle worship.

Worship cannot take place apart from redemption. This is illustrated graphically in the Old Testament event called the Exodus. What is the overarching theme of the book of Exodus? Jack Hayford wrote, "Exodus is primarily a study in the power of worship to release people … worship [is] at the center of Exodus."[4] Using Exodus 3 as his text, Hayford shows how that worship was at the heart of Moses' commission there at the burning bush and the core of the message the Lord told Moses to give to Pharaoh.

Worship was the issue in the power struggle between Pharaoh and God, the key to Israel's protection from the final plague, and the practical provision of nourishment for the first stage of their journey to the Promised Land. Worship was the destiny of this people, the center of their lives, and over and above all in the calendar the Lord outlined for them to follow.

The central theme of the book of Exodus is to illustrate that the purpose of redemption is worship. God said to Moses, "I will be with you. And this will be the sign to you that it is I who have sent you: When you have brought the people out of Egypt, *you will worship God* on this mountain" (Exodus 3:12 NIV, emphasis added). God's purpose in the Exodus event was to call out a special people—a kingdom of priests—to worship Him exclusively, and through their unique lifestyle of worship to become a witness to the world of God's power to deliver people from the bondage of sin.

In the same way that Hebrew worship was based in the retelling of the historical salvation event called the Exodus, New Testament worship, fulfilling that Old Testament type, is based on the historical salvation event called the gospel: the virgin birth, the vicarious death, and the victorious resurrection of Jesus Christ.[5] Worship is impossible apart from the finished work of Christ on the cross. This is the theme of the following great Philippian hymn:

> Let this mind be in you which was also in Christ Jesus, who, being in the form of God, did not consider it robbery to be equal with God, but made Himself of no reputation, taking the form of a bondservant, and coming in the likeness of men. And being found in appearance as a man, He humbled himself and became obedient to the point of death, even the death of the cross. Therefore God also has highly exalted Him and given Him the name which is above every name, that at the name of Jesus every knee should bow, of those in heaven, and of those on earth, and of those under the earth, and that every tongue should confess that Jesus Christ is Lord, to the glory of God the Father. (Philippians 2:5-11)

These great redemptive themes are dramatically retold every time we gather to worship. For example, we worship on the first day of the week to reenact and celebrate the fact that Jesus rose again on that day. In observing Christian baptism and the Lord's Table, we act out the death, the burial, and the resurrection of Christ in anticipation of His soon return. As the offering is being given, we are acting out that "God so loved the world, that He gave His only begotten Son" (John 3:16), and in response to His gift, we are inspired to give ourselves as living sacrifices, holy, acceptable to God, which is our reasonable service of worship (Romans 12:1-2). A right theology of worship is basic to our understanding of God's purpose in our redemption.

A Right Theology of Worship Is Biblical

We do not approach God on our terms. We come to Him at His invitation. David Peterson wrote, "the worship of the living and true God is essentially *an engagement with him on the terms that he proposes and in the way that he alone makes possible* [emphasis in original]."[6] It is revealing that I have found it easier to find "how-to" books on "doing" worship than books setting forth a biblical theology of worship. I am concerned that in the excitement and enthusiasm of the wonderful "praise and worship" revival sweeping the world today that we may be majoring on being "in spirit" and minoring on being "in truth." That was exactly the mistake Cain made in his approach to worship.

Could it be that much of what we offer up to God as worship today is so much "fruits and vegetables" that make us feel "worshipful" but in reality is not Christian worship at all, but mere self-gratification?

Our personal opinions about what constitutes effective worship are immaterial. God is not impressed with our "creative" worship. He was not impressed with the "creative" worship of Cain, who brought a bloodless sacrifice; or of King Saul, who refused to completely obey the Lord; or of Aaron's sons, Nadab and Abihu, who offered strange fire before the Lord. As a result of their offering unauthorized worship before God, contrary to His instruction, God destroyed Nadab and Abihu by a fire that "went out from the Lord" (Leviticus 10:2). Moses then explained to Aaron what had happened, "This is what the LORD spoke, saying: 'By those who come near Me I must be regarded as holy; and before all the people I must be glorified'" (Leviticus 10:3).

Please don't get me wrong. I am not against creativity or variety in worship. I'm simply saying that our first priority in worship should not be novelty, but adherence to biblical directives and guidelines. We can be as creative as we like within the boundaries God has set in His Word. God has clearly prescribed the manner in which He desires to be approached. We are arrogant indeed to believe we can improve upon God's plan. "Jesus said to him, 'I am the way, the truth, and the life. No one comes to the Father except through Me'" (John 14:6). Access to God is narrow and exclusive. We come to Him in worship on His terms and by His means. Only as we are grounded in a solid biblical theology of worship can we approach a holy God in the way that is acceptable to Him.

A right theology of worship must be *balanced* between spirit and truth. A right theology of worship is *basic* to our understanding of God's purpose in our redemption. A right theology of worship must be *biblical* if it is to be acceptable to God. This is why the study of the theology of worship is so crucial for us today.

Chapter 4

Worship's Past: History of Worship

What are all histories but God manifesting himself?

—Oliver Cromwell

*Worship … is giving to the Lord the glory that
is due in response to what he has revealed to
us and done to us in Jesus Christ his Son.*

—Oswald B. Milligan

His eyelids fluttered as he struggled to regain consciousness. Painfully, he rolled over and propped himself up on one elbow to look around. He discovered that he was lying in an alley surrounded by trash cans and debris. By the nasty bump on the back of his head, he surmised that he must have tripped and fallen and been knocked unconscious. With great difficulty, he rose to his feet and stood there for a moment to get his bearings. As he walked towards the street, fear and panic overwhelmed him as he realized that he could not remember where he was going or even who he was. He frantically searched his pockets for some clue as to his identity, only to discover that his wallet had been stolen. For some time he wandered around Toronto confused and bewildered, not knowing where to go or what to do. Exhausted, he finally sat down on a bench next to the walkway in front of City Hall. He smiled a rather puzzled smile at the man sitting next to him.

"Do we know each other?" asked Pastor A. W. Tozer.

"No, I don't think so," the young man replied. Then he added, "I think I'm in some sort of a jam."

He paused. "Something has happened to me. I think I tripped and fell somewhere in the city and bumped my head. I can't remember anything for sure. When I woke up, I had been robbed. My wallet and all of my cards and papers were gone. I have no identification—and I don't know who I am."

After they talked for a moment, Pastor Tozer was about to recommend that the young man go to the police station for help when he noticed a distinguished-looking gentleman standing next to them on the sidewalk. The gentleman had a confused expression on his face as he looked intently at the young man sitting next to Pastor Tozer. Recognizing the young man on the bench, he let out a sudden, delighted shout—almost a scream. He called his friend by name as he grabbed him and shook his hand.

"Where have you been and what have you been doing? Everyone in the orchestra is worried sick about you."

The lost man, still confused, replied, "Pardon me, sir, but I do not know you. I do not recognize you."

"What? You do not know me? We came to Toronto together three days ago. Don't you know that we are members of the philharmonic and that you are the first violinist? We have filled our engagement without you, and we've been searching everywhere for you."

"So that is who I am," he said with a shaky sigh of relief, "and that is why I am here!"[1]

Many Evangelicals today, like the young concert violinist, are wandering around confused and aimless with no sense of who they are, where they have been, or where they are going when it comes to their worship traditions. Consequently, because they have no recollection of their past, they have no foundation upon which to build their future, and they become stagnant and stale, locked in the present.

An Understanding of Worship History Is Foundational

Many Christians today feel that their public worship has little relevance to their daily lives. They have become bored, discontented, and restless because of the lack of creativity, the philosophy that worship is Christian entertainment, and with the polarization of worship styles between "all mind" and "all emotion."[2] One of the reasons for this phenomenon, says Robert Webber, is the anti-historical bias prevalent among many Evangelicals today.

> The problem with this attitude is that the rejection of historical perspective imprisons a movement within its present culture. This imprisonment results in the uninformed normalizing of the present moment in history, together with all its aberrations and shortcomings, and leads to a suspicious attitude toward the legitimate use of historical insights … Studying the origins of Christian worship supplies the key to overcoming negative results of historical amnesia. Anyone who desires to achieve worship renewal must pay attention to the sources and development of Christian worship.[3]

Our God is a God who acts historically. History has often been said to be "His story." The Hebrew people of the Old Testament were one of the first people groups to record their history, dramatically documenting God's intervention in the historical events of their lives personally and nationally. They believed that history gave meaning to their present and hope for their future. Their worship traditions were rooted firmly in their history, remembering God's acts of deliverance and provision while looking to the future for the fulfillment of God's promise of a coming Messiah. The psalmist wrote, "I will *remember* the works of the LORD; surely I will *remember* Your wonders of old" (Psalm 77:11, emphasis added). Likewise, in the New Testament, we hear Jesus say, "Do this in *remembrance* of me" (Luke 22:19, emphasis added).

Looking back to the historical event called Passover, Jesus not only gave meaning to the present, but also hope for the future when He said, "For I say to you, I will not drink of the fruit of the vine until the kingdom of God comes" (Luke 22:18). We cannot have an anti-historical mind-set and call it "Christian," when we are encouraged time and time again in God's Word to remember. Paul said to Timothy, "If thou put the brethren in *remembrance* of these things, thou shalt be a good minister of Jesus Christ, nourished up in the words of faith and of good doctrine" (1Timothy 4:6 KJV, emphasis added).

A historical perspective is critical to sound doctrine. Scripture cannot be rightly understood in a vacuum, but must be considered in its historical context. The same is true in the study of our worship heritage. We cannot know who we are if we do not know who we were. Peter wrote, "For this reason I will not be negligent to *remind* you always of these things, though you know and are established in the present truth" (2 Peter 1:12, emphasis added). Truth for the present can only be established on a historical foundation as we remember what God has done and what God has said in days gone by.

An Understanding of Worship History Is Educational

An understanding of Christian worship can be found by studying two primary sources: the Word of God and the history of the church. The two must be taken together, as neither can be properly understood apart from the other.

Since Pentecost, the Holy Spirit has been at work instructing, encouraging, and energizing the church throughout the ages. We can learn a great deal from how the church of God, led by that self-same Spirit, has perceived and practiced the biblical principles of worship down through the ages. For instance, we who are of the free-church tradition must be careful in our attitude toward worship history, that we do not discount the work of the Holy Spirit in the pre-Reformation period out of hand. I think in some cases the early reformers did exactly that, and in their zeal to correct some of the more blatant heresies in the medieval church caused the pendulum to swing to the opposite and equally dangerous extreme.[4]

It is especially important to study the worship practices of the early church during the first centuries because of the church's chronological nearness to the apostolic tradition and the church's commitment to continue "steadfastly in the apostles' doctrine" (Acts 2:42). It can be assumed that the closer we get to the worship practices of those men who were eyewitnesses to Christ's earthly ministry, the closer we can get to what real New Testament worship was like. That is not to say that we should take this historical information and put it on equal footing with scriptural authority, but the two will complement each other for a better understanding of what the New Testament teaches about biblical worship.[5]

In fact, it could be said that the Reformation itself was the result of adopting a historical-scriptural approach to worship. The Reformers, outraged by the decay and depravity of the late medieval church, purposed to reform worship to coincide more closely with what they believed were worship practices based in Scripture and the experience of the early disciples.[6] For the contemporary evangelical to resist an appreciation of worship history is to resist the very impetus of the Reformation itself—it is to deny our very identity. An understanding of worship history is not only foundational and educational; it is also interrelational.

An Understanding of Worship History Is Interrelational

Since the Reformation, many different worship traditions have evolved. All around us is proof that our God is a great lover of variety. Instead of promoting ecumenicalism at the expense of our doctrinal integrity, we should celebrate our diversity. James White wrote, "This means that the worship experiences of other traditions must be accorded respect and we must seek to understand others in order to know ourselves better."[7]

As you study the history of worship over the last twenty centuries, you will discover many similarities between your worship practices and that of other Christians around the world. You will be amazed at the similarities in things like the order of worship (liturgy) you use compared to that of other faiths. That really should come as no surprise, considering our common roots. We are more interrelated in our worship origins and practices than we might think. Our own worship experiences will become richer and more enjoyable when we come to appreciate the enormous breadth and depth of our common origins.

We are worshipping God today, not only with the Christians of the twenty-first century in which we live, but also with the millions around the throne who have gone on before. We are who we are as worshippers today because of the men and women who, for twenty centuries, have given us such a rich heritage of faith. We can learn from their mistakes, most certainly, but we can also be inspired by their devotion. Studying worship history is foundational, it is educational, and it is interrelational. Like the story of the young violinist demonstrates, it is in the study of worship history that we find out who we are and why we are here.

Chapter 5

Worship's Pattern: Tabernacle Worship

The New is in the Old concealed.
The Old is by the New revealed.

—St. Augustine

A young soldier, along with about fifty others, was sitting in the office of President Lincoln waiting to see the president. Back in those days, it was relatively easy to gain an audience with the commander-in-chief, as it was simply a matter of showing up and waiting your turn.

While the soldier was waiting, a little boy named Tad came around, and noticed the man in his uniform, and was especially fascinated by the armless sleeve pinned to the young man's shoulder. Tad, as you would expect of any little boy, asked a lot of questions, and the young soldier obliged by sharing some exciting stories from the war. After a while, Tad asked the soldier why he was there. He replied that he had come to see the president. Tad said, "The president is my father. Do you want to see my father?" The soldier said, "Yes." Tad said, "I will get you in," and without even knocking, slipped through the door to his father's office.

About that time the president's secretary came into the waiting room to inform those still there that the president would not be able to see anyone else that afternoon. Everyone got up to leave, except the young soldier boy. The secretary, not sure the young man had understood, repeated his announcement and told him it would be useless to wait any longer, to which he replied, "The president's son was here, and he has gone in to see his father to ask if I may come in."

The secretary said, "You mean little Tad?"

"Yes."

"Is he in with his father now?"

"Yes."

"Well, you will get in to see the president all right. If the president's son is there to plead for you, you wait; you'll get in."[1]

Like that young soldier boy we, too, have a similar problem when it comes to worshipping a thrice-holy God; and that is the problem of access. We have indeed been created for worship "but [our] iniquities have separated [us] from [our] God; and [our] sins have hidden His face from [us], so that He will not hear" (Isaiah 59:2).

In the Garden of Eden, before the Fall, man had a threefold privilege: he had access to God, he had the knowledge of God, and he was spiritually alive. But when man sinned, he lost it all. He lost access to God, he lost the knowledge of God, and he died spiritually. The good news is that everything man lost in the Garden because of the first Adam, he regained in the Second Adam. We see this outlined so simply in John 14:6 when Jesus said of Himself, "I am the way, the truth, and the life."

> Jesus is the way—our access to the Father. That is the doctrine of *reconciliation*. "No one comes to the Father except through me." (John 14:6)

> Jesus is the truth—by him we regain the knowledge of God. That is the doctrine of *illumination*. "He who has seen Me has seen the Father." (Jn. 14:9)

> Jesus is the life. That is the doctrine of *regeneration*. "For as in Adam all die, even so in Christ all shall be made alive." (1 Corinthians 15:22)

God used the tabernacle in the wilderness to teach these truths about the coming Christ to His chosen people and to help them understand that worship is impossible apart from the shed blood of "the Lamb of God who takes away the sin of the world" (John 1:29). This is seen even more clearly in the tabernacle's design.

In studying the construction of the tabernacle, we are made painfully aware that it is extremely difficult to get to the Holy of Holies where the manifest presence of God abides. Many barriers are constructed between the sinner and the *Shekinah*. We first encounter the linen curtain separating the people from the outer court. There is only one entrance, emphasizing the exclusiveness of access. After entering the eastern gate, we must stop at the brazen altar and then the laver. Once we arrive at the tabernacle itself, we find our passage blocked again by the curtain at the entrance of the sanctuary—the Holy Place. As we pass by the candlestick on the left and the table of showbread on the right, we come upon the altar of incense before the beautiful veil that separates us from the Holy of Holies. Here, God ordained that only one man could ever witness the wonder of the mercy seat and the glory of the *Shekinah* of God dwelling between the wings of the cherubim—the high priest himself—and then only once a year.

As Creatures created for worship, we have burning deep in our soul, a yearning to worship Him, and yet we cannot. Because of sin we are separated from God and denied access to Him—frustrated at every turn. But then, as we look around, we notice that there is blood everywhere. Every piece of furniture—every item—is stained with blood.

> For when Moses had spoken every precept to all the people according to the law, he took the blood of calves and goats, with water, scarlet wool, and hyssop, and sprinkled both the book itself and all the people, saying, *"This is the blood of the covenant which God has commanded you."* Then likewise he sprinkled with blood both the tabernacle and all the vessels of the ministry. (Hebrews 9:19-21, emphasis added)

We are reminded that "without shedding of blood there is no remission" (Hebrews 9:22). We begin to sense our utter helplessness and hopelessness at ever being in God's presence to release that pent-up yearning to worship our Creator. But then, finally, after hundreds of years and millions of sacrifices, as the writer of Hebrews states,

> But Christ came *as* High Priest of the good things to come, with the greater and more perfect tabernacle not made with hands, that is, not of this creation. Not with the blood of goats and calves, but with His own blood He entered the Most

Holy Place once for all, having obtained eternal redemption. (Hebrews 9:11-12)

When Christ cried, "It is finished," and commended his spirit to the Father, the veil, a type of the body of Christ separating the Holy Place from the Holy of Holies, was rent in two from top to bottom to announce that truly the ultimate price for sin had been paid in full. "Therefore, brethren, having boldness to enter the Holiest by the blood of Jesus, by a new and living way which He consecrated for us, through the veil, that is, His flesh" (Hebrews 10:19-20). At long last, we now have access to the Father. "Not by works of righteousness which we have done, but according to His mercy He saved us, through the washing of regeneration and renewing of the Holy Spirit, whom He poured out on us abundantly through Jesus Christ our Savior" (Titus 3:5-6).

The emphasis of the tabernacle is that Jesus is the essence of our worship. Every individual part of the tabernacle reveals a different facet of Christ's character as it relates to our worship of the Father, as follows:

Jesus is the Door: our invitation. Jesus said, "I am the door. If anyone enters by Me, he will be saved." (John 10:9)

Jesus is the Brazen Altar: our imputation. "But we see Jesus, who was made a little lower than the angels, for the suffering of death crowned with glory and honor, that He, by the grace of God, might taste death for everyone." (Hebrews 2:9)

Jesus is the Laver: our purification. "Husbands, love your wives, just as Christ also loved the church and gave Himself for her, that He might sanctify and cleanse her with the washing of water by the word, that He might present her to Himself a glorious church, not having spot or wrinkle or any such thing, but that she should be holy and without blemish." (Ephesians 5:25-27)

Jesus is the Candlestick: our illumination. "Then Jesus spoke to them again, saying, 'I am the light of the world. He who follows Me shall not walk in darkness, but have the light of life.'" (Jn. 8:12)

Jesus is the Showbread: our sustentation. "And Jesus said to them, 'I am the bread of life. He who comes to Me shall never hunger, and he who believes in Me shall never thirst.'" (John 6:35)

Jesus is the Incense: our supplication. "Therefore He is also able to save to the uttermost those who come to God through Him, since He always lives to make intercession for them." (Hebrews 7:25)

Jesus is the Mercy Seat: our propitiation. "Being justified freely by His grace through the redemption that is in Christ Jesus, whom God set forth *as* a propitiation by His blood." (Romans 3:24-25)

As you study the tabernacle, you will understand more clearly Christ's mission of providing us access to the Father though His blood, that we might once again fulfill the purpose for which we were created—the worship of God. As Paul wrote, "Therefore, having been justified by faith, we have peace with God through our Lord Jesus Christ, through whom also we have access by faith into this grace in which we stand, and rejoice in hope of the glory of God" (Romans 5:1-2).

Charles Wesley's Good Friday hymn based on John 19:30 says it so well.

'Tis finished! The Messiah dies,
Cut off for sins, but not His own.
Accomplished is the sacrifice,
The great redeeming work is done.

The veil is rent; in Christ alone
The living way to heav'n is seen;
The middle wall is broken down,
And all the world may enter in.

The types and figures are fulfilled;
Exacted is the legal pain;
The precious promises are sealed;
The spotless Lamb of God is slain.

The reign of sin and death is o'er,
And all may live from sin set free;
Satan has lost his mortal pow'r;
'Tis swallowed up in victory.[2]

Chapter 6

Worship's Power:
Praise and Worship

*The worship of the New Testament ... is nothing
else than song, praise, and thanksgiving. This is a
unique song. God does not care for our sacrifices and
works. He is satisfied with the sacrifice of praise.*

—Martin Luther

John writes in Revelation 19:6, "And I heard, as it were, the voice of a great multitude, as the sound of many waters and as the sound of mighty thunderings, saying, 'Alleluia! For the Lord God Omnipotent reigns!'" The word *alleluia*, which literally means, "praise the LORD," is pronounced the same in every language around the world, as if to encourage the whole of mankind to lift their voices in unison in praise to a thrice-holy God. George Frederick Pentecost, an associate of D. L. Moody and Ira Sankey, once said,

> I am profoundly sure that among the divinely ordained instrumentalities for the conversion and sanctification of the soul, God has not given a greater, besides the preaching of the gospel, than the singing of psalms and hymns and spiritual songs. I have known a hymn to do God's work in a soul when every other instrumentality has failed. I have seen vast audiences melted and swayed by a single hymn when they have been unmoved by a powerful presentation of the gospel from the pulpit.[1]

The story of King Jehoshaphat is a wonderful biblical example of music's effectiveness as a tool of worship and praise, especially as it relates to spiritual warfare. First of all, let's look at …

The Power of Praise

King Jehoshaphat in 2 Chronicles 20 had just received word that a great army was coming against Judah from the land of Moab and Ammon. He immediately called the nation together to pray and fast before the Lord. Standing in the midst of all those assembled there at the temple in front of the new courtyard, he began to pray earnestly to God on their behalf. As he closed his prayer, he said, "O our God, will You not judge them? For we have no power against this great multitude that is coming against us; nor do we know what to do, but our eyes *are* upon You" (2 Chronicles 20:12).

As Jehoshaphat was praying, God had already prepared His answer. While the King was yet speaking, God heard and sent his reply by the prophet Jahaziel, whose name literally means, "whom Jehovah watches over." Jahaziel was a Levite, one of the sons of Asaph, which would have made him one of the singers of praise. Through Jahaziel, God would remind Judah that He was watching over them. Jahaziel began to prophesy, "Do not be afraid nor dismayed because of this great multitude, for the battle is not yours, but God's. You will not need to fight in this battle. Position yourselves, stand still and see the salvation of the Lord" (2 Chronicles 20:15, 17).

Jehoshaphat gathered his generals together and formed a council of war. How did they prepare for this battle? Did they map out an intricate battle strategy? Did they prepare their swords and sharpen their spears? No! Instead they organized, of all things, a great praise choir to lead the army into battle. After Jehoshaphat organized the singers in front of the troops, he instructed them in what they were to sing, "Praise the LORD; for His mercy endures forever" (2 Chronicles 20:21). And so, with this audacious advance against the enemy, Jehoshaphat demonstrated his firm reliance upon God and God alone.

God's Word tells us that as they began to praise the Lord, God sent an ambush against the Moabites and the Ammonites, and for some unknown reason, they turned on one another and did not rest until every last man among them was killed. When the army of Judah, lead by that great praise choir, arrived at the battlefield, they found to their great amazement, that the whole multitude lay dead on the ground. When God's people began the work of praise, God began the work of deliverance.

As we look closer at this exciting story, we can see ...

The Pattern of Praise

First, *Jehoshaphat recognized his problem.* He humbly brought his nation to God and confessed his utter helplessness and hopelessness apart from God's intervention. And so by faith, *Jehoshaphat relied on prayer.* When he heard of the encroaching forces, his first response was not to muster his military might but to call the nation of Judah to prayer and fasting. Years later, the Apostle Paul would write, "Be anxious for nothing, but in everything by prayer and supplication, with thanksgiving, let your requests be known unto God" (Philippians 4:6).

And so, in that prayer, *Jehoshaphat requested God's protection.* Although he had a great disciplined army, he did not rely on his own strength, but instead looked to the hand of God for deliverance. Because he recognized his problem, relied on prayer, and requested God's protection, *Jehoshaphat responded with praise.* Even before the battle was fought, by faith, he began to praise the Lord. Jehoshaphat believed that "if God be for us, who can be against us?" (Romans 8:31). His faith gave him the assurance of things hoped for and the conviction of things not seen (Hebrews 11:1). He was so confident in God's ability to protect them, that in Jehoshaphat's mind, the battle was as good as won. Jehoshaphat offered God a sacrifice of praise, and God was pleased, so much so, that *Jehoshaphat reaped God's provision.*

Jehoshaphat and his armies, led by the praise choir, reached the valley there at En Gedi where the enemy was encamped. As they topped the summit and looked down on the field of battle, their mouths gaped open in astonishment to see the valley filled with the dead bodies of their enemies. With wonder and awe, they began to gather the spoils of war: cattle, tents, clothing, horses, harnesses, tapestries, gold, silver, and precious stones. So great was the bounty, it took them three whole days just to gather it all up; even then, it was still too much for them to carry.

No doubt you could have heard the sound of that great chorus echoing in triumph again down through the valley, "Praise the LORD; for His mercy endures forever!" Without a doubt, praise is powerful!

We've observed the power of praise, we've learned the pattern of praise, now let's look at …

The People of Praise

After Jahaziel prophesied God's promise of deliverance to King Jehoshaphat and the people of Judah, Scripture says that

> Jehoshaphat bowed his head with *his* face to the ground, and all Judah and the inhabitants of Jerusalem bowed before the LORD, worshipping the LORD. Then the Levites of the children of the Kohathites and of the children of the Korahites stood up to praise the LORD God of Israel with voices loud and high. (2 Chronicles 20:18-19)

Notice that no one was excluded from praising the Lord. It is appropriate for everyone and everything at all times to praise the Lord. That theme is recapitulated throughout Scripture. In Psalm 74:21, the poor and needy are encouraged to praise the Lord. In Psalm 148:12, the young and the old should praise the Lord. In that same verse, both men and women are also to praise the Lord. In Psalm 67:5, "Let the peoples praise You, O God; Let all the peoples praise You." In Psalm 148:2, "Praise Him, all His angels." In Psalm 148, the sun, the moon, and the stars are to praise Him; dragons, fish, and animals are to praise Him; hail, snow, and the birds of the air are all to praise the Lord. Again and again David would repeat the refrain, "Oh that men would praise the LORD for his goodness, and for his wonderful works to the children of men!" (Psalm 107:8, 15, 21, 31).

Paul and Silas sang praise in prison at the midnight hour. A song of praise echoed across the Red Sea as walls of water fell on the forces of Pharaoh. When Deborah and Barak had defeated the armies of Sisera, a song of praise was sung. Mary presented to God a Magnificat of praise when she heard of the coming Christ child. Even Jesus and His disciples, on that fateful night before His crucifixion there in the upper room, sang praise together.[2]

Before time began, Job tells us that the "morning stars sang together" (Job 38:7) in praise to an almighty God. The early church praised the Lord. The church today continues to praise the Lord, and into the eons of eternity, the heavens will ring as the church triumphant rends the rarefied air of glory with the song of Moses and the Lamb (Revelation 15:3). Down through the ages, one generation after another has been bound together by a golden cord of praise.

Who are the people of praise? Who should praise the Lord? Hear King David's clarion call, "Let everything that has breath praise the LORD. Praise the LORD!" (Psalm 150:6).

Now that we've seen the people of praise, let's look at the object of our adoration. Consider with me now ...

The Person of Praise

John wrote,

> Before anything else existed, there was Christ with God. He has always been alive and is Himself God. He created everything that there is. Nothing exists that He didn't make. All that came to be was alive with His life, and that life was the light of men. (Jn. 1:1-4 TLB)

Before the dawn of time, before the first sunrise slipped over majestic mountain peaks, before the first star twinkled in the heavens above, Jesus was. Jesus Christ—God of very God. Jesus Christ—man of very man. Jesus Christ—God and man in one person, and so, He is worthy of our praise.

As a man, Jesus grew weary, but as God He said, "Come to Me, all *you* who labor and are heavy laden, and I will give you rest" (Matthew 11:28). As a man, He got hungry, but as God He fed thousands with a young boy's lunch. As a man, He got thirsty, but as God He offered the woman at the well living water to drink. As a man, He prayed, but as God, He made, in prayer, no confession of sin. As a man, He slept, but as God, He awoke from sleep and stilled the storm and calmed the waves. As a man, He accepted an invitation to a village girl's wedding, but as God, He there turned the water into wine. As a man, He wept at the tomb of His friend Lazarus, but as God He raised Lazarus from the dead.[3]

The Jews in John 5:18 sought to slay Christ because He had the audacity to call God His Father, making Himself equal with God. As Jesus defended His deity with the wisdom of the Word and the logic of the Logos of God, He said, "You search the Scriptures, for in them you think you have eternal life; and these are they which testify of Me" (John 5:39). The written Word of God we hold in our hands is nothing less than a hymnal of praise to the living Word of God—the Lord Jesus. We can see His portrait in every precious page, as follows:

In Genesis, Jesus is the ram at Abraham's altar. In Exodus, He's the Passover lamb. In Leviticus, He's our great high priest. In Numbers, He's the cloud by day and the pillar of fire by night. In Deuteronomy, He's our city of refuge.

In Joshua, He's the captain of the Lord's hosts. In Judges, He's our righteous judge. In Ruth, He's our kinsman redeemer. In 1 Samuel, He's our trusted prophet. In 2 Samuel, He's the princely king. In 1 Kings, He's David's choice. In 2 Kings, He's the holiest of all. In 1 Chronicles, He's king by birth. In 2 Chronicles, He's king by judgment. In Ezra, He's our faithful scribe. In Nehemiah, He's the rebuilder of everything that's broken. In Esther, He's Mordecai sitting faithful at the gate.

In Job, He's our Redeemer who ever lives. In Psalms, He's the shepherd who supplies our every need. In Proverbs, He's our wisdom. In Ecclesiastes, He's the preacher. In Song of Solomon, He's the beautiful bridegroom.

In Isaiah, He's our Immanuel, the Wonderful Counselor, the Mighty God, the Everlasting Father, the Prince of Peace. In Jeremiah, He's the Lord our righteousness. In Lamentations, He's the weeping prophet. In Ezekiel, He's the wonderful four-faced man. In Daniel, He's the fourth man in the midst of the fiery furnace.

In Hosea, He's my love that is forever faithful. In Joel, He's the Holy Spirit baptizer. In Amos, He's our burden bearer. In Obadiah, He's our Savior. In Jonah, He's the risen prophet. In Micah, He's the messenger with beautiful feet. In Nahum, He's our avenger. In Habakkuk, He's the watchman ever praying for revival. In Zephaniah, He's the Lord mighty to save. In Haggai, He's the desire of all nations. In Zechariah, He's our fountain of forgiveness. In Malachi, He is the Son of Righteousness with healing in His wings.

In Matthew, He's the king of the Jews. In Mark, He's the suffering servant. In Luke, He's the perfect Son of Man. In John, He's the only begotten Son of God.

In Acts, He's the ascended Lord. In Romans, He's our justifier. In 1 Corinthians, He's our resurrection. In 2 Corinthians, He's our reconciliation. In Galatians, He's our liberty. In Ephesians, He's our unsearchable riches. In Philippians, He's our joy. In Colossians, He's the fullness of the Godhead bodily. In 1 and 2 Thessalonians, He's our soon-coming king. In 1 and 2 Timothy, He's the mediator between God and man. In Titus, He's our blessed hope. In Philemon, He's a friend who sticks closer than a brother. In Hebrews, He's the best of all.

In James, He's the great physician. In 1 Peter, He's the chief cornerstone. In 2 Peter, He's the Lord of glory. In 1 John, He's the way. In 2 John, He's the truth. In 3 John, He's the life. In Jude, He's the Lord coming with ten thousand saints, and in Revelation, "Alleluia! For the Lord God Omnipotent reigns! He is King of Kings and Lord of Lords!"[4]

John, being in the Spirit on the Lord's Day, wrote,

> Then I looked, and I heard the voice of many angels around the throne, the living creatures, and the elders; and the number of them was ten thousand times ten thousand, and thousands of thousands, saying with a loud voice:
>
> "Worthy is the Lamb who was slain
> To receive power and riches and wisdom,
> And strength and honor and glory and blessing!"
>
> And every creature which is in heaven and on the earth and under the earth and such as are in the sea, and all that are in them, I heard saying:
>
> "Blessing and honor and glory and power
> *Be* to Him who sits on the throne,
> And to the Lamb, forever and ever!" (Revelation 5:11-13)

Let us join with the millions gathered around God's throne and today begin to perfect that activity which will occupy our time for all eternity—singing praise to our risen and reigning Lord!

Chapter 7

Worship's Practice: The Heart of the Worship Leader

The church has always prospered most when
it has been blessed with strong and spiritual
leaders who expected and experienced the
touch of the supernatural in their service.

—J. Oswald Sanders

Planning and leading worship is at once a wonderful privilege and an awesome responsibility. There are many things that we could talk about related to worship planning and leading, but we must always start with the worship leader himself, because "the acceptability of any act of worship is determined by the acceptability of the worshipper."[1]

There are many excellent examples of effective worship leaders found in the pages of God's Word: Moses, Joshua, Nehemiah, David, Solomon, and many others. But of all the great worship leaders in Scripture, the most fascinating to me was John the Baptist, who I would submit was Christianity's first worship leader. I know that might initially strike you as a little strange. When we think of John the Baptist, we don't usually think of him in terms of being a worship leader, but Luke describes the job description of a worship leader in a nutshell when he describes the ministry of John the Baptist, "The voice of one crying in the wilderness: 'Prepare the way of the LORD; Make His paths straight. Every valley shall be filled and every mountain and hill brought low; the crooked places shall be made straight and the rough ways smooth'" (Luke 3:4-5).

It was customary in John's day that workmen would be sent out ahead of traveling royalty to prepare the road for the coming entourage. Ravines and gullies would be filled in, steep places would be knocked down, winding trails would be straightened and widened, and rough places would be smoothed out to make a highway upon which the dignitary could travel unimpeded. This is exactly the responsibility of a worship leader—to prepare the way for unimpeded worship.

Drawing from the worship-leading ministry of John the Baptist recorded in the four Gospels, I have isolated three basic principles that can be applied to the worship leader's ministry. First, a worship leader's ministry is preceded by a call; second, it is public in its character; and third, it is pure in its conduct.

A Worship Leader's Ministry Is Preceded by a Call

In the summer of 1967, I was attending a youth camp sponsored by our church's association at the Roman Nose State Park in Watonga, Oklahoma. Dennis Treat, a former missionary to Uruguay, was the camp pastor that year. Each morning and evening, he would lead us in a study of God's Word, challenging us with God's call upon our lives, not only to be saved but also to serve.

One night as we gathered around the campfire, I sensed God's call upon my life to the gospel ministry. I had just started playing the trumpet and had a keen interest in anything musical, so I believed God was calling me, specifically, to the music ministry. I stood from where I was sitting and at twelve years of age publicly responded to God's call upon my life. Immediately, God began to open doors of service as opportunities came to play my trumpet and sing in youth revivals and church services across our state. When I was fifteen, I accepted the call of Twin Oaks Baptist Church in Oklahoma City to be their minister of music, and I have been a minister of music ever since.

I will never forget that summer youth camp as long as I live, as that was the place and the time God called me out to serve him as a worship leader. At that moment my life was changed. The focus of my life intensified like a laser beam. Everything I have done since has been in preparation for what I am doing now and intend to do until Jesus comes—leading others to worship Him. From a study of the call of John the Baptist, I believe that God calls a worship leader to a threefold task—one of a prophet, one of a preacher, and one of a priest.

John the Baptist's Call Was Announced by Isaiah— He Was To Be a Prophet

How fitting that John the Baptist's call as a prophet was announced by a prophet. The verse previously quoted from Luke is actually the following quote from Isaiah:

> Prepare the way of the LORD; make straight in the desert a highway for our God. Every valley shall be exalted and every mountain and hill brought low; the crooked places shall be made straight and the rough places smooth; the glory of the LORD shall be revealed, and all flesh shall see *it* together; for the mouth of the LORD has spoken. (Isaiah 40:3-5)

The Old Testament prophet was both a foreteller and a *forth*-teller. His job was not to interpret God's will, but to simply deliver the message God had given him.[2] "The Old Testament prophet acted as a mouthpiece for God, receiving a message from Him and proclaiming it in accordance with His commands."[3] As the canon of Scripture neared completion, the role of the prophet began to change significantly. The New Testament prophet, like his Old Testament counterpart, also received a message from God, but over time received it more and more from the written Word and then, relying on the Holy Spirit, would make appropriate application to the church. Paul tells us that this prophetic word is to accomplish three specific purposes: "But he who prophesies speaks edification and exhortation and comfort to men" (1 Corinthians 14:3).

Genuine worship will be edifying.

The word translated "edification" is *oikodome* from *oikodomeo*, which means "to build a house." In this context, it has to do with building up the household of faith so that it can profit and advance spiritually.[4] Practically speaking, edification is concerned with teaching. Genuine worship will teach about the one being worshipped. This is vitally important because what a man knows about God—his doctrine—will affect how he worships God. As we gaze intently upon the Lord in worship, we cannot help but learn more of Him. We become like what we worship. The more the worshipper knows about God, the more he will love God and become like Him. As worship leaders, we must be careful that the words we use and the songs we sing in worship are doctrinally sound, because right doctrine always precedes right worship. A worship leader's prophetic roll will include edification.

Genuine worship will be exhorting.

The word translated "exhortation" is *paraklesis*, which is "the act of calling toward or hither to help, begging, and also of exhortation, encouragement toward virtue … the purpose of which is to strengthen faith."[5] In John 14:16, Jesus uses a similar word to refer to the Holy Spirit, designating Him as Paraclete.

> This new Paraclete, the Holy Spirit, was to witness concerning Jesus Christ (John 14:26; 16:7, 14) and to glorify Him. The Holy Spirit is called a Paraclete because He undertakes Christ's office in the world while Christ is away from the world as the God-Man. He is also called the Paraclete because He acts as Christ's substitute on earth.[6]

Worship that is led by the Holy Spirit will help the worshipper to become more like Christ and will encourage him to live a holy life. Worship strengthens and establishes us in our faith. As worship leaders we need to be reminded that worship cannot be a *paraklesis* (a help and an encouragement) unless we are depending upon the Paraclete (the Holy Spirit) in its planning and leading. A worship leader's prophetic roll will include exhortation.

Genuine worship will be consoling.

The word translated "comfort" is *paramuthia* and is derived from two words: *para,* near, and *muthos,* speech. It means to speak closely to anyone, denoting consolation, comfort with a great degree of tenderness.[7]

Worship comforts the believer. Jesus said, "Come to Me, all *you* who labor and are heavy laden, and I will give you rest" (Matthew 11:28). As we come to Christ in worship, we find rest for our weary souls. As worship leaders, we must be constantly aware that this comfort is not derived from our skill in delivering the message or presenting the music, as important as that may be, but is derived from the Master Himself. "Then the disciples were glad when they saw the Lord" (John 20:20). People are not made glad by just hearing a new song, or even by hearing another wonderful sermon, as much as I love good songs and good sermons. They are only made glad "when they see the Lord." When people leave a service of worship that we have led, if we have done our job well, they will not be talking about the great singer, or the great song, or even the great sermon, they will only be talking about the great Savior we have in Jesus Christ. John the Baptist understood this important principle of worship leadership when he said, "He must increase, but I *must* decrease" (John 3:30). In our planning and leading of worship we must always direct people's attention to Christ and away from ourselves if they are to find the comfort and peace they so desperately need. A worship leader's prophetic roll will include consolation.

These three prophetic qualities of worship leadership—edification, exhortation, and consolation—should be kept in mind as we plan and lead corporate worship, remembering that they are not necessarily goals to be achieved, but rather blessings that will be received as a result of genuine worship.

His Call Was Acclaimed by Gabriel— He Was To Be a Preacher

As John the Baptist's father was ministering in the temple, an angel appeared to him and said,

> Do not be afraid, Zacharias, for your prayer is heard; and your wife Elizabeth will bear you a son, and you shall call his name John. And you will have joy and gladness, and many will rejoice at his birth. For he will be great in the sight of the Lord, and shall drink neither wine nor strong drink. He will also be filled with the Holy Spirit, even from his mother's womb. And he will turn many of the children of Israel to the Lord their God. He will also go before Him in the spirit and power of Elijah, *"to turn the hearts of the fathers to the children,"* and the disobedient to the wisdom of the just, to make ready a people prepared for the Lord. (Luke 1:13-17)

It is interesting that an angel—an *aggelos*—acclaimed John the Baptist's call to his father because the Gospel of Mark refers to John the Baptist using a similar word. "As it is written in the Prophets: *'Behold, I send My messenger [aggelon] before Your face, Who will prepare Your way before You'"* (Mark 1:2). Much in the same way that John the Baptist's call as a prophet was announced by the prophet Isaiah, so John the Baptist's call as an *aggelon* (a messenger) was acclaimed by an *aggelos* (an angel) whose name was Gabriel.

The word *aggelos* means "messenger, to bring a message, announce, proclaim."[8] What was the message John the Baptist announced as he came out of the wilderness? It was the same message that Jesus proclaimed after His wilderness experience, "Repent, for the kingdom of heaven is at hand!" (Matthew 3:2). A worship leader's message will emphasize repentance.

John the Baptist was the key transitional figure between the work of the prophet in the Old Testament and the work of the prophet in the New Testament. Although the Old Testament rarely refers to what the prophets did as "preaching," they were indeed the preachers of their day. Their message was one of repentance, and their primary concern was the hypocrisy of God's people, who were orthodox in their outward worship practices but wicked and idolatrous in their hearts. The theme of repentance in John's message speaks of that heritage.

The transitional phrase in John's message was this: "For the kingdom of heaven is at hand" (Matthew 3:2). The first time "kingdom" is mentioned in the Bible is in a very definite worship connotation. God had just delivered Israel from Egyptian bondage and had brought them to Sinai to worship him. God said, "And you shall be to Me a kingdom of priests and a holy nation" (Exodus 19:6). Merrill Tenney says that the phrase "kingdom of God" can be understood as

> The sovereign rule of God manifested in Christ to defeat His enemies, creating a people over whom He reigns, and issuing in a realm or realms in which the power of His reign is experienced. All they are members of the kingdom of God who voluntarily submit to the rule of God in their lives. Entrance into the kingdom is by the new birth. (John 3:3-5)[9]

There at Sinai, Israel accepted God's kingship over them by voluntarily vowing to obey Him and worship Him exclusively. The idea of a kingdom ruled by the Messiah was not new to the Jews to whom John the Baptist preached. What was a new thought to them was the method by which one entered the kingdom.

The purpose of John the Baptist's ministry was "to make ready a people prepared for the Lord" (Luke 1:17), which is the purpose of our ministry as worship leaders as well. John the Baptist's mission was to introduce the "way" to the kingdom—Jesus Christ. Jesus is the kingdom. You cannot separate the kingdom from the King. To be in Christ is to be in the kingdom. Jesus said to Nicodemus, "unless one is born again, he cannot see the kingdom of God" (John 3:3). This is the moment of transition between the message of the Old Testament prophets and the message of the New. Matthew 11:13 says, "For all the prophets and the law prophesied until John." After John the Baptist a *new* message began to be preached. From John the Baptist on, the message preached was not simply "repent," but "believe the gospel." "The gospel began in John Baptist. His baptism was the dawning of the *Gospel day.*"[10] A worship leader's message will not only emphasize repentance, but will also emphasize the gospel.

Scripture, at this point begins to emphasize that in order to be born again—in order to enter the kingdom—you must believe the gospel. Paul declares that the gospel is the story of how "Christ died for our sins according to the Scriptures, and that He was buried, and that He rose again the third day according to the Scriptures" (1 Corinthians 15:3-4). The gospel is the virgin birth, the vicarious death, and the victorious resurrection of Jesus Christ. Although the events of the cross and the empty tomb had not yet been realized, I think John the Baptist had at least a limited understanding of the gospel, because on two different occasions he emphasized the sacrificial nature of Christ's work here on the earth. "The next day John saw Jesus coming toward him, and said, 'Behold! The Lamb of God who takes away the sin of the world!'" (John 1:29). And then the very next day, John, "looking at Jesus as He walked … said, 'Behold the Lamb of God!'" (John 1:36).

In the Old Testament, they were *waiting,* asking the question, "Where *is* the Lamb?" (Genesis 22:7). In the New Testament, they were *watching,* proclaiming, "Behold the Lamb." In the future around God's throne, we will be *worshipping,* singing, "Worthy is the Lamb!" (Revelation 5:12).[11] An effective worship leader will, like John, make much of the Lamb of God in his worship planning.

After His baptism, Jesus Himself emphasized this transition in the prophet's message as He went about preaching not only repentance, but also "the gospel of the kingdom."[12] The word *gospel* appears 101 times in the New Testament. Twenty-three references are made to "preaching the gospel," which is central to what we do in worship. It is the essence of worship itself. In fact, Robert Webber says, "Worship tells and acts out the life, death, resurrection, and coming again of Christ."[13] In planning and leading worship, we must always be sure that the gospel is preeminent in every service. Like John the Baptist, we must each week point men and women and boys and girls to Christ and say, "Behold! The Lamb of God who takes away the sin of the world!" That is the preaching aspect of a worship leader's call.

His Call Was Affirmed by Zechariah—He Was To Be a Priest

John the Baptist's father, Zachariah, was a priest, a descendant of Aaron. Not only was he a descendant of Aaron, but he was also of the house of David. "No families in the world were so honored of God as those of Aaron and David; with one was made the covenant of priesthood, with the other that of royalty."[14]

One day, according to the custom of the priesthood, it fell Zechariah's lot to minister in the temple burning incense before the Lord both morning and evening. In the course of his duties, an angel appeared to him standing on the right side of the altar of incense. Zechariah must have been scared to death because the angel said to him, "Do not be afraid, Zacharias, for your prayer is heard; and your wife Elizabeth will bear you a son, and you shall call his name John" (Luke 1:13). The angel went on to tell Zechariah what kind of man John would be.

After the angel delivered his amazing message, Zechariah was simply overwhelmed. He could not believe what he was hearing. He said to the angel, "How shall I know this? For I am an old man, and my wife is well advanced in years" (Luke 1:18). John the Baptist's parents—like the parents of Isaac, Jacob, Joseph, Samson, and Samuel—had been praying for a son for many years. Now they were too old to have children and evidently had given up on their request—but God had not forgotten. Because of Zechariah's unbelief, the angel, who now introduced himself as Gabriel, took away his ability to speak until the boy was born—that would be the sign Zechariah requested by which he would know these things that Gabriel was saying were true. After Zechariah had completed his duties at the temple, he went home to his wife. And just as Gabriel had predicted, Elisabeth became pregnant.

Nine months later, Elisabeth was delivered of a beautiful baby boy. On the eighth day, the family and friends gathered to celebrate the ritual of circumcision at which time the boy would officially be given his name. They assumed he would be named after his father, but Elisabeth, knowing of the angel's instructions, said, "No; he shall be called John" (Luke 1:60). Since there was no one by that name in the family, those gathered turned to Zechariah, who was still unable to speak, to see if he agreed. He called for a writing tablet and wrote, "His name is John." At that moment, his tongue was loosed, and with great joy and full of the Holy Spirit, he prophesied concerning the ministry of his son,

> And you, child, will be called the prophet of the Highest; for you will go before the face of the Lord to prepare His ways, to give knowledge of salvation to His people by the remission of their sins, through the tender mercy of our God, with which the Dayspring from on high has visited us. (Luke 1:76-78)

Zechariah, the priest, affirmed his son John's call to a priestly ministry—a ministry that involved preparing the Lamb who would take away the sin of the world. We can learn much from John the Baptist that will help us to understand the priestly roll of a worship leader, but first, let's lay some foundation.

After their deliverance from Egypt, just as He had promised Moses at the burning bush, God brought Israel to Mount Sinai to worship Him and there offered them a unique role among the nations of the earth as a "kingdom of priests" (Exodus 19:6). They foolishly declined this offer, so God chose to bestow the honor of the priesthood upon the tribe of Levi generally and the house of Aaron exclusively as the high priest, setting them apart as ministers before the Lord. At the same time, tabernacle worship was instituted as a means of preaching the gospel of the coming Christ to the Jews, using ritual and symbolism until such time as the Christ would atone for sin once and for all.

The most important privilege of the Old Testament high priest was that of access to God. He alone could enter the Holy of Holies behind the veil, and then only once a year. When Christ died on the cross, becoming at once the sacrificial Lamb of God and the Great High Priest, the veil in the temple that separated the Holy Place from the Holy of Holies was rent in two from top to bottom. Hebrews 10:20 explains that this veil, which had for hundreds of years prevented access to God, was actually a type of Christ's sinless human body. Jesus, the Great High Priest, having paid the penalty for sin once and for all with His own blood, removed "the middle wall of partition" (Ephesians 2:14 KJV) and gave us, at long last, access to the very throne of God.

Because of Christ's death upon the tree, we who are in Christ share in His priesthood, giving us direct access to the Father without the need of a human intermediary. This describes the doctrine commonly referred to as the "priesthood of the believer."

> You also, as living stones, are being built up a spiritual house, a holy priesthood, to offer up spiritual sacrifices acceptable to God through Jesus Christ ... But you *are* a chosen generation, a royal priesthood, a holy nation, His own special people, that you may proclaim the praises of Him who called you out of darkness into His marvelous light. (1 Peter 2:5, 9)

Peter says that our responsibility as believer-priests is "to offer up spiritual sacrifices, acceptable to God through Christ Jesus." There are at least four spiritual sacrifices that we can offer to God as believer-priests: ourselves, our song, our substance, and our service.

We should offer the sacrifice of ourselves.

Romans 12:1 says, "I beseech you therefore, brethren, by the mercies of God, that you present your bodies a living sacrifice, holy, acceptable to God, *which is* your reasonable service [of worship]."

Notice the *request* that Paul makes of us—a request founded in the mercy of God: "I beseech you therefore, brethren, by the mercies of God." God in His mercy has saved us. God in His mercy has secured us.

God in His mercy has sustained us. He is more than justified in making this request.

Notice the *requirement:* "You present your bodies a living sacrifice, holy, acceptable unto God." We are to make this sacrifice *unilaterally: "you present."* The word translated "present" is *paristemi*, which means "to yield."[15] To yield is to give or render as fitting, rightfully owed, or required; it is to give up possession of upon claim or demand; to surrender or submit oneself to another.[16] The apostle Paul wrote,

> Or do you not know that your body is the temple of the Holy Spirit *who is* in you, whom you have from God, and you are not your own? For you were bought at a price; therefore glorify God in your body and in your spirit, which are God's. (1 Corinthians 6:19-20)

It is indeed most fitting that we should yield our bodies to Christ. Our unilateral presentation of our lives to Him is what is rightfully owed in light of His own sacrifice for us that purchased our redemption.

We are to make this sacrifice *unconditionally:* "You present your bodies a living sacrifice." In Old Testament worship, when the sacrifice would begin to cook on the altar over the flame, the muscle would begin to draw and twist and turn over the heat. There was the potential that the sacrifice could become desecrated by twisting and turning itself off the altar, so God instructed Moses that two meat hooks be fashioned for the priests to use in keeping the sacrifice *tied down.* I believe that the two meat hooks that keep you and me, as living sacrifices, *tied down* upon the altar of service are discipline and devotion.

Over the years, as I have invited people to serve in one area of ministry or another, I would often hear them say something like this, "Oh, I'd like to sing in the choir, but you know, you guys rehearse every week and you sing every Sunday—I just don't want to get *tied down."* "Oh, I'd like to teach a class, I know I should, I know I could, but I'd have to study every week and it would make it hard to go out of town whenever I wanted—I just don't want to get *tied down."* "Oh, I'd like to do this or that for the Lord, but I *want* to be free to do what I *want* to do, when I *want* to do it—I just don't want to get *tied down."*

It is much more difficult to be a living sacrifice than it is to be a dead one. Dead sacrifices feel no pain. That's why when the fire gets hot and ministry becomes uncomfortable, inconvenient, and difficult, we feel like we just can't take the heat and we're tempted to roll off the altar, but when that happens its discipline and devotion that keep us *tied down.*

We are to make this sacrifice *uncompromisingly:* "Holy, acceptable unto God, which is your reasonable service." The Old Testament priest would not have even dared offer God a partial sacrifice. For a sacrifice to be acceptable, it had to be whole and given completely. If what we do for God is to be holy, it must be given wholly, that is, uncompromisingly. As believer-priests, we have a duty to offer to God a sacrifice of ourselves unilaterally, unconditionally, and uncompromisingly.

We should offer the sacrifice of our song.

Hebrews 13:15 says, "Therefore by Him let us continually offer the sacrifice of praise to God, that is, the fruit of *our* lips, giving thanks to His name." Watchman Nee said, "We must not only raise the note of praise when we stand on the summit and view the promised land of Canaan, but we must learn to compose psalms of praise when we walk through the valley of the shadow of death. This is truly praise."[17]

Paul and Silas, having been beaten within an inch of their lives and cast into the darkest, dankest part of the dungeon; with their feet clamped in leg irons; battered, bloodied, and bruised; lifted their voices at the midnight hour in a concert of prayer and praise for all the prisoners to hear. As a result of that midnight worship service, the earth quaked, prison doors were opened, chains were loosed, and the jailer and his entire family came to faith in Christ. It is easy indeed to praise God when all is well and life is grand, but real praise—praise that is sacrificial—is praise offered at the midnight hour. There is nothing quite as impressive to a lost world as sacrificial praise. It is a powerful witness and a worthy offering to the Lord.

We should offer the sacrifice of our substance.

Hebrews 13:16 says, "But do not forget to do good and *to share*, for with such sacrifices God is well pleased" (emphasis added). Here the believer-priest is encouraged to offer a sacrifice that involves his personal possessions, especially as it relates to helping others.

A wonderful biblical example of sacrificial giving is found in Paul's love letter to the church at Philippi. Paul is imprisoned in Rome on trial for his life. Having heard of his situation, the church at Philippi wanted to send something to the great apostle that would encourage him and remind him that they were thinking about him and praying for him. In those days, there was no Federal Express or UPS. If you wanted to send something to someone, you had one of three choices: take it yourself, wait for someone who was going that way, or hire someone to do it for you. However, there was in the church, a charming fellow, named Epaphroditus (his name literally means "charming"), who volunteered to take the gift on behalf of the church. As a result of his sacrificial service, he became very sick and nearly lost his life.

Paul made this recommendation to the church regarding Epaphroditus: "Receive him therefore in the Lord with all gladness, and hold such men in esteem" (Philippians 2:29). In fact, the entire book of Philippians is a thank-you note from the apostle, carried back by Epaphroditus, to express Paul's gratitude for the precious sacrificial gift given by the church to meet Paul's physical need. Paul writes,

> Indeed I have all and abound. I am full, having received from Epaphroditus the things *sent* from you, a sweet-smelling aroma, an acceptable sacrifice, well pleasing to God. And my God shall supply all your need according to His riches in glory by Christ Jesus. (Philippians 4:18-19)

Paul, using the beautiful worship imagery of the altar of incense, describes their gift as a sweet smell that rises to God as an acceptable sacrifice. In these two verses, Paul is saying to the church, "You have been faithful to meet my need; in like manner, God will be faithful to meet your needs according to His riches in glory by Christ Jesus." God is pleased when we give sacrificially to the needs of others.

We should offer the sacrifice of our service.

Look again at Hebrews 13:16, "But do not forget to *do good* and to share, for with such sacrifices God is well pleased" (emphasis added). Someone has said, "Great opportunities to help others seldom come, but small ones surround us every day."[18] As worship leaders, what we do in service to others on Christ's behalf during the week energizes what we do on the platform on Sunday. We need to search out these opportunities to "do good," as they are acts of worship that honor God.

Jesus said, "Assuredly, I say to you, inasmuch as you did *it* to one of the least of these My brethren, you did *it* to Me" (Matthew 25:40b). Worship leading, in its priestly function, offers the sacrifices of self, song, substance, and service. But that's not all. As believer-priests we are called not only to offer sacrifice, but to also be a priestly intercessor.

An important function of the priest was to intercede on the behalf of others before God. First Timothy 2:1 says, "Therefore I exhort first of all that supplications, prayers, intercessions, *and* giving of thanks be made for all men." Part of our daily worship time should be concerned with interceding to the Lord on the behalf of those we lead in worship each week. As we become aware of the spiritual needs of the individuals and families in our congregation, the Holy Spirit will help us in our worship planning to emphasize the appropriate character qualities of God that will minister to those specific needs. To the weak, we can emphasize that He is El Elyon—the strongest strong one; to the misunderstood, He is El Roi—the strong one who sees. For those bewildered and confused, He is Jehovah-Raah—the Lord my shepherd. To the lonely, He is Jehovah-Shamma—the Lord who is present. To the destitute, He is Jehovah-Jireh—the Lord who provides. To the sick in body and heart, He is Jehovah-Rapha—the Lord who heals.

Right doctrine is so important to right worship. What we know about God affects how and to what depth we are able to worship Him. Paradoxically, as a result of God-centered worship, heartfelt personal needs will be met as we, with understanding, worship Him.

I hope that our study so far has helped us to understand that our calling as a worship leader is much deeper, much wider, and much higher than most of us have imagined. A worship leader's ministry is preceded by a call—a call to be a prophet, a preacher, and a priest.

A Worship Leader's Ministry Is Public in Its Character

Matthew records, "In those days, John the Baptist came preaching in the wilderness of Judea" (Matthew 3:1). The word translated "came" is *paraginomai*, which means *"to appear publicly."*[19] A worship leader's ministry by definition is very public. Peter said, "Knowing this first, that no prophecy of Scripture is of any private interpretation" (2 Peter 1:20). The gospel was never meant to be hidden in a corner, but shouted from the housetops.

Paul reminded King Agrippa of the public nature of the gospel: "For the king, before whom I also speak freely, knows these things; for I am convinced that none of these things escapes his attention, since this thing was not done in a corner" (Acts 26:26). The Scripture commended Apollos "for he vigorously refuted the Jews *publicly*, showing from the Scriptures that Jesus is the Christ" (Acts 18:28, emphasis added). Paul, addressing the Ephesian elders, said, "I kept back nothing that was helpful, but proclaimed it to you, and taught you *publicly* and from house to house" (Acts 20:20, emphasis added). Every disciple that Christ called, He called publicly. Jesus said,

> You are the light of the world. A city that is set on a hill cannot be hidden. Nor do they light a lamp and put it under a basket, but on a lampstand, and it gives light to all *who are* in the house. Let your light so shine before men, that they may see your good works and glorify your Father in heaven. (Matthew 5:14-16)

From the life of John the Baptist, we will learn that a public ministry requires three things: preparation, prayer, and personality.

A Public Ministry Requires Preparation.

After Zechariah prophesied that his son would "be called the prophet of the Highest," and that God would use him to prepare the way for the Lord, the Scripture says of John the Baptist, "So the child grew and became strong in spirit, and was in the deserts till the day of his manifestation to Israel" (Luke 1:80). Many times in God's Word, the desert was used as a place of preparation and testing. The Greek word translated "desert" is the word *eremos*, which speaks not so much of the desert's dryness as it does the desert's loneliness and solitude.[20]

Moses needed preparation

Moses, once a prince of Egypt, had been living on the backside of the Sinai desert for forty years as a fugitive. At eighty years of age, something extraordinary happened that changed his life forever.

> Now Moses was tending the flock of Jethro his father-in-law, the priest of Midian. And he led the flock to the back of the desert, and came to Horeb, the mountain of God. And the Angel of the LORD appeared to him in a flame of fire from the midst of a bush. (Exodus 3:1-2)

It was in the desert, tending his father-in-law's sheep all those years, that Moses learned meekness and humility. It was there that God prepared him to lead Israel out of Egyptian bondage into the Promised Land. I've heard my dad say that Moses spent his first forty years in Pharaoh's palace, learning how to be a somebody; he spent the next forty years on the backside of the desert, learning how to be a nobody; and then he spent the last forty years of his life, learning what God can do with a man who has learned the first two lessons.

Vance Havner wrote,

> It is always on the backside of the desert that we come to the mountain of God, on the backside of the desert of self, at the end of our own dreams and ambitions and plans. Moody said that when Moses first undertook to deliver Israel he looked this way and that way (Exodus 2:12) but when he came back from Horeb he looked only one way, God's way. But before he saw God's way he had to come to the backside of the desert.[21]

Moses was prepared for ministry in the desert.

The Israelites needed preparation.

God led Israel to wander in the desert for forty years to prepare them for the conquest of Canaan.

> Then it came to pass, when Pharaoh had let the people go, that God did not lead them *by* way of the land of the Philistines, although that *was* near; for God said, "Lest perhaps the people change their minds when they see war, and return to Egypt." So God led the people around *by* way of the wilderness of the Red Sea. (Exodus 13:17-18)

The children of Israel did not come out of Egypt as a nation of warriors, but rather as a nation of slaves. Had they gone right to the Promised Land from Egypt, they would have been eaten alive by the land and its inhabitants, because they were totally unprepared for the task before them. The desert taught them to rely upon God; it toughened them up in spirit, body, and character. Moses even wrote a song about it.

> He found him in a desert land
> And in the wasteland, a howling wilderness;
> He encircled him, He instructed him,
> He kept him as the apple of His eye. (Deuteronomy 32:10)

The Israelites were instructed by God and prepared for what lay before them in the desert.

Jesus needed preparation.

After Jesus' baptism, the Scripture says he was led to the desert to fast and pray for forty days. "Then Jesus was led up by the Spirit into the wilderness to be tempted by the devil" (Matthew 4:1). It was there in the Judean wilderness that He was prepared specifically for the wilderness temptations as well as for the great work that lay before Him. Many times after that, Jesus would go out into a desert place to commune with God and refresh His spirit. He taught His disciples, "Come aside by yourselves to a deserted place and rest a while" (Mark 6:31). It was out in the desert that Jesus taught the multitudes, fed the thousands, and instructed His disciples. Jesus was prepared for ministry in the desert.

John the Baptist needed preparation.

No doubt, John the Baptist received intense training at the knee of his father, Zechariah, as it was not uncommon for a priest to prepare his son for the priestly duties he would begin upon reaching adulthood. But how much more diligently would Zechariah have prepared this boy, knowing his calling as a prophet, a priest, and a preacher and the prophecy concerning him: "The voice of one crying in the wilderness: 'Prepare the way of the LORD; Make straight in the desert a highway for our God'" (Isaiah 40:3).

Though he must have learned much from his father; it was there in the desert where God began to hammer out a mighty prophet. It was there in the lonely place, after his mother and father had died, that God became his Father—nurturing him, sustaining him, teaching him, and giving him the dogged determination to stand flat-footed against the leaders of his day and cry out with unmitigated courage, "Repent! For the kingdom of heaven is at hand" (Matthew 3:2). John was prepared for ministry in the desert.

If Moses, the Israelites, Jesus, and John the Baptist needed preparation for ministry, what does that say about you and me? As worship leaders, we need to "come aside" for a while; we need to hide in the desert; we need to spend some "lonely" time with God, preparing our spirits and our skills to become more effective worship leaders.

I tell my worship studies students at Liberty University that every person who has answered God's call to ministry will eventually find themselves in the desert. There will come a time when you will feel that God has forsaken you, that you are all alone, and that no one cares. Dryness, discouragement and disappointment will overwhelm you. The sultry, stifling, scorching heat of ministry will sap you of your strength and evaporate once plentiful resources. You will be tempted to give up, to give in, and to give out. But I am here today to tell you not to despair! God is in the desert! He has not forsaken you; He is preparing you for your greatest days of ministry just ahead. Moses learned that after the desert was deliverance. The Israelites learned that the wilderness wandering was the way to the Promised Land. It was after the desert that "Jesus returned in the power of the Spirit to Galilee" (Luke 4:14). And in the case of John the Baptist, it was in the desert that he discovered his destiny as "the voice of one crying in the wilderness: 'Prepare the way of the LORD'" (Luke 3:4).

I remember hearing the story told about an old lumberjack who was looking for a job at a logging company. The old man claimed that he could chop down more trees in a day than anyone else. They put him to the test against the camp's best lumberjack—a young, big, strong, Paul-Bunyan-type. It was almost comical seeing the two men standing there side by side—one so young, big and strong and the other so old, small and comparatively frail. All bets were on the young logger as the gun was fired and the contest began.

The other loggers cheered their champion as the young lumberjack began to cut down trees for all he was worth. He never stopped but feverishly chopped and chopped. The old man also began in earnest, but everyone laughed, as he had to stop often to rest. When it came time at the end of the day to tally the results, everyone was shocked and amazed to learn that the old man had won. They could not believe it, but the proof was undeniable. They asked the old man, "How did you do it? How could you chop so much wood when you stopped so often to rest? The old man laughed and replied, "I wasn't resting. I was sharpening my ax."

My dad used to encourage me to get as much education as possible. He would always say, "Son, you can cut a lot more wood with a sharp ax than you can with a dull one." A man who has prepared well for his ministry will accomplish so much more over a longer period of time than the man who has not. There is no time lost in taking time to prepare.

A Public Ministry Requires Prayer

It matters not how talented we are, how educated we might be, or how much experience we may have, nothing we do in public ministry will be of any eternal value if it is not the product of persevering prayer. James wrote, "The effective, fervent prayer of a righteous man avails much" (James 5:16b). We find a clue in Luke 11 that John the Baptist was just such a man. "Now it came to pass, as [Jesus] was praying in a certain place, when He ceased, *that* one of His disciples said to Him, 'Lord, teach us to pray, *as John also taught his disciples*'" (Luke 11:1, emphasis added). Today, we think of John the Baptist as a fiery prophet and a bold preacher, but during his day, he was also known for being a great man of prayer. You remember John's father was a man of prayer, and as a result of his prayer, God gave him a son in his old age. Zechariah must have taught his boy how to pray.

Look closely at the request of Jesus' disciples. They wanted to learn how to pray "as John taught his disciples." Jesus replied by teaching them what we now call the Lord's Prayer. I wonder in this context how much of the Lord's Prayer may have actually been John's prayer. At any rate, the prayer that Jesus taught his disciples must have had many similarities to the way John prayed.

During my college days, I started a little routine at the end of every semester that became a precious time to get alone with God. On the day of my last semester exam, my wife, Donnita, would help me pack a little red and blue gym bag with enough clothes for two or three days. As soon as I finished the last exam, I would drive directly from school down to the Arbuckle Mountains, where I had reserved a room at our state youth campground. It was a precious time. No television, no telephone, no people—just God and me. I would take my Bible and walk out into the hills where I had found a beautiful place by a little stream that ran through the middle of the encampment. There I would talk to God, meditate on His Word, and allow the Holy Spirit to recharge my batteries.

If we really want to experience the mighty power of God upon our ministry, we are going to have to get away more often into the desert, like John, for the express purpose of being alone with God. Jesus' disciples could not understand why they could not help the lunatic boy who would often cast himself into the fire. Jesus sternly rebuked them, saying, "However, this kind does not go out except by prayer and fasting" (Matthew 17:21).

I have become intensely aware that I must spend more time in prayer if I am going to be the worship leader God wants me to be. Vance Havner said, "The devil is in constant conspiracy against a preacher who really prays, for it has been said that what a minister is in his prayer closet is what he is, no more, no less."[22] It is the height of arrogance to think that we can do God's work without God's power—and that power comes only by prayer. J. Oswald Sanders wrote,

> The purposes of the Pentecostal filling were eminently practical. The apostles were faced with a superhuman task for which nothing less than supernatural power would avail. The fullness of the Spirit imparted the power they needed for the truceless warfare to which they were committed. (Luke 24:29; Ephesians 6:10-18)[23]

I read of a church that had just purchased a beautiful pipe organ at great expense. They were all so very proud of this new majestic instrument, and this was the formal dedication day. The auditorium was packed with eager worshippers anxious to hear the first great chords fill the church with praise. Just as the organist was lifting his hands to come down on the keyboard, the electricity went out on the console. Immediately, an electrician was summoned. As the electrician worked feverishly to restore the power, the minister of music led in some *a cappella* congregational singing. At last, the electrician had the problem figured out, and during the prayer, he handed a note to the organist that read, "After the prayer, the power will be on."[24] The application to the life of the worship leader is obvious. If we want to have the power of God on our ministry, then we must become men and women of prayer.

> There is a place where thou canst touch the eyes
> Of blinded men to instant, perfect sight;
> There is a place where thou canst say, "Arise"
> To dying captives, bound in chains of night;
> There is a place where thou canst reach the store
> Of hoarded gold and free it for the Lord;
> There is a place—upon some distant shore—
> Where thou canst send the worker and the Word.
> Where is that secret place—thou dost ask, "Where?"
> O soul, it is the secret place of prayer!
>
> —Alfred Lord Tennyson

A Public Ministry Requires Personality

A public ministry requires preparation and prayer, but it also requires personality. This is a difficult subject to approach, but the fact is, personality has a great deal to do with one's success and effectiveness as a worship leader. I think it would be an understatement to say that John the Baptist had a lot of personality. "Then Jerusalem, all Judea, and all the region around the Jordan went out to [see John] and were baptized by him in the Jordan, confessing their sins" (Matthew 3:5-6). The scripture says that the whole region of Jordan came out to take a look at this unusual man.

> John's character, his asceticism, his strange, solitary life, his stern, awful, heart-stirring preaching, commanded attention … The wilderness was lonely no more; it was filled with thronging crowds. There was an attraction not to be resisted in his preaching. Men could not help but come; they could not help but listen.[25]

Webster's defines *personality* as "the totality of an individual's behavioral and emotional tendencies … the organization of the individual's distinguishing character traits, attitudes, or habits."[26] In the Old Testament, the Hebrew word *sem* most closely resembles this concept of personality and is most often translated "name."

> Thus the sum total of a person's internal and external pattern of behavior was gathered up into his name. In this way, one could give honor to the person of God (Psalm 5:11; 7:17). Knowing the name of a person was equivalent to knowing his essence, for the believing "know the name" of their God (Psalm 9:10; 91:14) … One's existence in his earthly form was bound in with his name. When the name had been destroyed, the man had for all intents and purposes also been dealt a deathblow. What else does a man actually own, in the last analysis, beside his personality? To have these things is to have the man.[27]

Gabriel was very explicit that Zechariah's little boy should be given a certain name. "You shall call his name John" (Luke 1:13). John's name means "Jehovah is gracious." John's name—his personality—would be a testament to God's grace in sending the Lamb of God who would take away the sin of the world.

Like John the Baptist, God purposefully caused you to be born *when* he wanted you to be, *where* he wanted you to be, and to *whom* he wanted you to be born. He has allowed every circumstance of your life, both good and bad, in order to shape and mold your unique personality. God has a purpose for your life and has fitted you with the basic personality to best accomplish that purpose. Even more wonderful is the fact that at our spiritual birth God has given each of us a "new" name (Revelation 2:17). We have been named with Christ. We are Christians. We have taken on the personality—the name—of Christ. This name change is highly significant.

> To change the name was to imply a change in the character and mission … Not only does the changing of the name indicate the close ties that the name has with the person and his personality but the person was so intimately connected with his name that "to cut off the name" was tantamount to cutting off the man.[28]

Upon receiving Christ, we immediately take on a new nature and begin the process of allowing the attitude—the personality—of Christ to be manifest in our lives. "Therefore, if anyone *is* in Christ, *he is* a new creation; old things have passed away; behold, all things have become new" (2 Corinthians 5:17).

There are many different models in use today to help us get a handle on this concept of personality. Many businesses and schools administer personality tests of different kinds, realizing that a person's personality has a lot to do with his potential for success in a particular kind of employment or ministry. The advantage of having this information is to help us evaluate our strengths and weaknesses in order to keep growing as a person and make improvements that will make us more effective in ministry.

Many people, when confronted with a personality flaw, fall into the old trap of saying, "Well, that's just the way I am." For the believer, that clichéd excuse no longer holds water. For the Christian, when it comes to our personality, the emphasis is no longer on "the way I am" but rather on the way Christ is. The question we should be asking ourselves is, "Am I allowing the personality of Christ to be lived out in me?" The best way to develop your personality spiritually is to spend a great deal of time in worship because the more we spend time with Christ the more like Him we become.

> Worship liberates the personality by giving a new perspective to life, by integrating life with the multitude of life-forms, by bringing into the life the virtues of humility, loyalty, devotion and rightness of attitude, thus refreshing and reviving the spirit.[29]

The goal of every believer should be to become more like Christ. That is God's ultimate goal for every one of us. Romans 8:29 tells us that conformity to Christ is the "good" that Paul mentions in Romans 8:28, "And we know that all things work together for good to those who love God, to those who are the called according to *His* purpose. For whom He foreknew, He also predestined *to be* conformed to the image of His Son." The psalmist says, "As for me, I will see Your face in righteousness [that's worship]; I shall be satisfied when I awake in Your likeness [that's the result]" (Psalm 17:15).

Paul discusses biblical personality development in Philippians 2:3-11: "*Let* nothing *be done* through selfish ambition or conceit, but in lowliness of mind let each esteem others better than himself. Let each of you look out not only for his own interests, but also for the interests of others." In verse five He presents the Lord Jesus as the perfect picture of this selfless, submissive, servant spirit, imploring us to let the attitude—the "mind"—of Christ Jesus be in us. He then recounts for us the seven-fold, self-humbling of Christ as an example to follow: (1) He left heaven's glory, (2) He made himself of no reputation, (3) He was made in the likeness of man, (4) He took upon himself the form of a servant, (5) He humbled himself, (6) He became obedient unto death, and (7) He died on a cursed cross.[30]

A whole book could be written about the personality of the worship leader, but for the purposes of this study, suffice it to say that our highest priority should be to acquire the mind—the attitude—the personality of Christ. A worship leader's ministry is public in its character and requires preparation, prayer, and personality in order to be effective and enduring.

A Worship Leader's Ministry Is Pure in Its Conduct

Not only is a worship leader's ministry preceded by a call and public in its character, it is also pure in its conduct. There are three things we can learn from the purity of John's conduct that will help us to have spiritual power in leading worship: John the Baptist was consecrated, common, and commended.

John the Baptist Was Consecrated

The angel Gabriel told John's father that John would be a Nazarite from his mother's womb: "For he will be great in the sight of the Lord, and shall drink neither wine nor strong drink. He will also be filled with the Holy Spirit, even from his mother's womb" (Luke 1:15). The law of the Nazarite was given to Moses by the LORD in Numbers 6:1-21. The Hebrew word *Nazarite* can be translated "consecrated" and can be defined as follows:

> [A nazarite was] an Israelite who consecrated himself or herself and took a vow of separation and self-imposed abstinence for the purpose of some special service. The Nazarite vow included a renunciation of wine, prohibition of the use of the razor, and avoidance of contact with a dead body. The period of time for the vow was anywhere from 30 days to a lifetime (Numbers 6:1-21; Judges 13:5-7; Amos 2:11-12).[31]

As John the Baptist was consecrated to God in his ministry, so should we be in ours. Holiness is the primary prerequisite for spiritual power. Jerry Bridges gives us an excellent definition of what it means to be holy. "To be holy is to be morally blameless. It is to be separated from sin and, therefore, consecrated to God. The word signifies 'separation to God, and the conduct befitting those separated.'"[32] Peter tells us why this is so important. "But as He who called you *is* holy, you also be holy in all *your* conduct, because it is written, *'Be holy, for I am holy'*" (1 Peter 1:15-16).

It seems like the older I get the more like my father I become. I cannot help but laugh out loud sometimes when I catch myself talking or gesturing like him. No doubt about it, I am my father's son. In like manner, the older we get in Christ, we should more and more catch ourselves behaving like the Father. If our heavenly Father is anything, He is holy, so we should be holy as well. James said, "Pure and undefiled religion before God and the Father is this: to visit orphans and widows in their trouble, *and* to keep oneself unspotted from the world" (James 1:27).

Like the Nazarite who would not touch death, drink wine, or cut his hair, so we must separate ourselves from the dead things of this world, abstain from the intoxicating temptations of a world system set against God, and not allow anything into our lives that would cut off the power and strength that derives from the power of the Almighty. A. W. Tozer observed,

> No one whose senses have been exercised to know good and evil can but grieve over the sight of zealous souls seeking to be filled with the Holy Spirit while they are living in a state of moral carelessness and borderline sin. Whoever would be indwelt by the Spirit must judge his life for any hidden iniquities. He must expel from his heart everything that is out of accord with the character of God as revealed by the Holy Spirit … There can be no tolerance of evil, no laughing off the things God hates.[33]

If we are going to have power in leading worship we must be consecrated—we must "lay aside every weight, and the sin which so easily ensnares *us*" (Hebrews 12:1). A worship leader's ministry should be consecrated.

John the Baptist Was Common

I use the word *common* to describe John's humble and unpretentious nature. I see his humility in his appetite, his appearance, and his attitude toward Christ.

Notice John's humility in his appetite.

"Now John … ate locusts and wild honey" (Mark 1:6). Here we see a subtle indication of John's humility in the simple things he ate. Locusts and wild honey were permitted to be eaten (Leviticus 11:22), but it was food eaten by the common people. Locusts are eaten even today in the Holy Land, but they are considered to be a common and inferior food. "They are a sign of temperance, poverty, and penitence."[34] John could say with the psalmist, "Do not incline my heart to any evil thing, to practice wicked works with men who work iniquity; and do not let me eat of their delicacies" (Psalm 141:4). John's appetite was a testimony to his singleness of heart and his sincere humility.

Notice John's humility in his appearance.

"Now John was clothed with camel's hair and with a leather belt around his waist" (Mark 1:6). John was not a hypocrite. His walk matched his talk. He was a prophet, and his appearance was consistent with his calling. He was not pretentious. He was not canvassing for office. He was not trying to impress people with himself; his concern was to impress people with Christ. Paul, writing to the Corinthians said, "For we do not commend ourselves again to you, but give you opportunity to boast on our behalf, that you may have *an answer* for those who boast in appearance and not in heart" (2 Corinthians 5:12). There should be nothing about our appearance that would distract from our message. Vance Havner wrote,

> One does not have to be a psychiatrist to read marks of vicious temper, hidden resentment, evil thoughts. They show in the droop of the mouth, the wrinkled forehead, the glint in the eye. Abraham Lincoln once objected to a certain appointment because he did not like the candidate's face. Someone interposed, "But Mr. President, a man cannot help how he looks." Mr. Lincoln replied: "He can't help how he looks when he comes into this world but he can help how he looks after forty years."[35]

Our appearance should point men to Jesus and be consistent with our message.

Notice John's humility in his attitude.

We can observe John's humility in his attitude toward Christ. "And he preached, saying, 'There comes One after me who is mightier than I, whose sandal strap I am not worthy to stoop down and loose'" (Mark 1:7). It was the job of the slave to help remove the shoes from his master's feet, but here, in great humility, John the Baptist says that he is not worthy to even be Christ's slave. Later, John compared Jesus to the bridegroom and himself to the best man. "He who has the bride is the bridegroom; but the friend of the bridegroom, who stands and hears him, rejoices greatly because of the bridegroom's voice. Therefore this joy of mine is fulfilled. He must increase, but I *must* decrease" (John 3:29-30). As George Whitefield said, "Let my name be forgotten, let me be trodden under the feet of all men, if Jesus may thereby be glorified."[36] That is the heart of the true worship leader. A worship leader's ministry should be common.

John the Baptist Was Commended

Near the end of John the Baptist's ministry, he was thrown in prison for daring to confront King Herod with the sin of adultery. While he was there in prison, I think he became discouraged and may have allowed himself to entertain his doubts about who Jesus was, because when he heard of the many wonderful things Jesus was doing, he sent two of his disciples to ask Jesus if He was indeed the Messiah. Jesus encouraged them by itemizing His messianic credentials as prophesied in Isaiah 29:18 and 35:4-6. After John's disciples had left, Jesus began to speak to the people gathered around concerning John. He summed up his commendation of John with these words, "Assuredly, I say to you, among those born of women there has not risen one greater than John the Baptist" (Matthew 11:11). A worship leader's ministry should be commended.

We have learned from the life of John the Baptist that the worship leader's ministry is preceded by a call, is public in its character, and is pure in its conduct. Leading worship is the most precious privilege in the world, but that privilege is overshadowed by its tremendous responsibility. John

69

the Baptist took his responsibility of pointing men to Christ very seriously, as should we.

One of the great leaders of the Salvation Army was Samuel Logan Brengle. He had the following tremendous insight into real spiritual leadership:

> It is not won by promotion, but by many prayers and tears. It is attained by confessions of sin, and much heart searching and humbling before God; by self-surrender, a courageous sacrifice of every idol, a bold, deathless, uncompromising and uncomplaining embracing of the cross, and by an eternal, unfaltering looking unto Jesus crucified. It is not gained by seeking great things for ourselves, but rather, like Paul, by counting those things that are gain to us as loss for Christ. That is a great price, but it must be unflinchingly paid by him who would be not merely a nominal but a real spiritual leader of men, a leader whose power is recognized and felt in heaven, on earth and in hell.[37]

If we are faithful to our calling as a worship leader in the way that John the Baptist was, we have the promise that we, too, will be commended for a job well done. God has endowed us with certain talents that he expects us to nurture and invest. We must be careful that we do not bury them or abuse them, but rather use them in leading men, women, boys, and girls to worship the King of Kings and Lord of Lords. If we have done this, we can expect to hear Jesus say, "Well *done,* good and faithful servant; you were faithful over a few things, I will make you ruler over many things. Enter into the joy of your lord" (Matthew 25:21).

Chapter 8

Worship's Priority: Lifestyle Worship

Every situation of life is a call to worship.

—Dr. Tom Elliff

In this climactic chapter in our study of Christian worship, we will seek to make practical application of all we've learned so far. We will come to understand what it means to worship God as a lifestyle day-by-day and moment-by-moment. We will learn that every situation of life is a call to worship. The Apostle Paul said it this way, "For to me, to live *is* Christ" (Philippians 1:21). He expands on this theme of lifestyle worship in his epistle to the Romans:

> Therefore, I urge you, brothers, in view of God's mercy, to offer your bodies as living sacrifices, holy and pleasing to God—this is your spiritual act of worship. Do not conform any longer to the pattern of this world, but be transformed by the renewing of your mind. Then you will be able to test and approve what God's will is—his good, pleasing and perfect will. (Romans 12:1-2 NIV)

Notice these three key phrases in Romans 12:1: "spiritual act of worship," "God's mercy," and "living sacrifices." The idea of "spiritual act of worship" reminds us of the connection between worship and spiritual warfare; the idea of "God's mercy" reminds us of the connection between worship and our redemption; and the idea of "living sacrifices" reminds

71

us of the connection between worship and our call to discipleship. These three ideas—spiritual warfare, redemption, and discipleship—are all interrelated to one another and are included in the concept of lifestyle worship.

Romans 12:1-2 outlines for us the following three foundational truths: the *prize* of spiritual warfare is worship, the *purpose* of redemption is worship, and the *process* of discipleship is worship. These three ideas taken together will help us understand the tremendous breadth and depth of lifestyle worship.

You cannot discuss lifestyle worship without first discussing spiritual warfare. They are inextricably linked, and may by synonymous, because "a worshipping church must of necessity be a warring church, for true worship is spiritual warfare."[1]

Once we understand the connection between spiritual warfare and worship, we can better understand the purpose of God's redemptive plan that was put into motion as a result of the angelic conflict, which was where spiritual warfare began. We will see that the issue at stake in the angelic conflict was worship. One of the eventual results of that conflict was man's decision to ignore God's instruction regarding the Tree of the Knowledge of Good and Evil and, in effect, make a decision to "worship" Satan.

To worship someone or something, by definition, is "to attribute worth" to the object of worship.[2] Adam and Eve attributed more worth to what Satan said than to what God had said. They failed to exclusively worship God at that point, and immediately, Satan took advantage of the situation and seized control of the world that had been man's God-given dominion (Genesis 1:26).

Because of man's sin in failing to worship God exclusively there in the Garden of Eden, there needed to be a plan by which man could be reconciled to God so that unhindered worship could be restored and the angelic conflict resolved. In a word, that plan is called "Grace." David Peterson commented, "In the 'Song of Zechariah,' we are told that the whole purpose of the messianic redemption is to enable God's people to worship or serve him."[3] The specific reference is found in Luke 1:74: "To grant us that we, being delivered from the hand of our enemies, might serve Him without fear."

Once we realize that the purpose of our redemption is to restore us to our place as worshippers before God, we are ready to understand that the means by which we become more like Christ is also through worship. In fact, the term "lifestyle worship" is just another way to say "discipleship." The aim of discipleship is to become more like Christ. Paul said, "Let this mind [this attitude] be in you which was also in Christ Jesus" (Philippians 2:5). The biblical approach to effective discipleship is worship.

With that quick overview of my argument, let's look at each point in more detail.

The Prize of Spiritual Warfare is Worship

James writes,

> Where do wars and fights *come* from among you? Do *they* not *come* from your *desires for* pleasure that war in your members? You lust and do not have. You murder and covet and cannot obtain. You fight and war. Yet you do not have because you do not ask. (James 4:1-2)

Wars always start because two parties each want the same thing. The story is told of a neighbor in Springfield, Illinois, who heard children crying outside his home. Upon opening his door to investigate, he saw Abraham Lincoln with his two sons, both of them throwing a fit. "What is the matter with the boys?" asked the man. Lincoln replied, "Just what is the matter with the whole world! I have three walnuts and each boy wants two."[4]

In all the discussions I have heard or read concerning spiritual warfare, no one ever mentions what is really being fought over. What is the issue? What is the battle all about? If we don't know what the prize is, how will we know if it has been won? I believe from a study of God's Word that the prize of spiritual warfare is worship—Satan desires it, but only God deserves it. It is easy to understand that worship is the prize in spiritual warfare when we see the tremendous effort Satan has used and will use to acquire it. Satan desired worship in heaven, in the Garden, in the desert, and *will* desire worship in the temple during the Tribulation.

Satan Desired Worship in Heaven

Following is the biblical record of that fact:

> How you are fallen from heaven, O Lucifer, son of the morning!
> *How* you are cut down to the ground, you who weakened the
> nations! For you have said in your heart: "**I will** ascend into
> heaven, **I will** exalt my throne above the stars of God; **I will**
> also sit on the mount of the congregation on the farthest sides
> of the north; **I will** ascend above the heights of the clouds, **I
> will** be like the Most High." (Isaiah 14:12-14, bolded emphasis
> added)

In this passage, we discover the headwaters of sin and rebellion and
the beginning of the angelic conflict described in Revelation 12:7-9:

> And war broke out in heaven: Michael and his angels fought
> with the dragon; and the dragon and his angels fought, but
> they did not prevail, nor was a place found for them in heaven
> any longer. So the great dragon was cast out, that serpent of
> old, called the Devil and Satan, who deceives the whole world;
> he was cast to the earth, and his angels were cast out with him.

The reason for the rebellion can be clearly seen by following the five
"I will" statements uttered by Satan and summed up in the last phrase
in Isaiah 14:14, "I will be like the Most High." Satan's desire to "be like the
Most High" refers to his covetousness of the worship that is God's and
God's alone. D. E. Hiebert said, "In his ambition to assume the place of
God, Satan is mastered by a consuming passion to receive worship as
God."[5] Warren Wiersbe agrees:

> Many scholars believe that Isaiah 14:12-15 goes beyond the
> immediate reference to the king of Babylon and applies to
> Satan. If so, then a desire for worship (which is basically pride)
> was the sin that brought about Lucifer's fall. "I will ascend
> above the heights of the clouds, I will be like the Most High"
> (Isaiah 14:14). Apparently, a number of angelic creatures were
> willing to worship Lucifer, and they fell with him.[6]

Indeed, Satan instigated the angelic conflict in heaven for the purpose
of usurping God's authority, ascending His throne, and receiving worship.

Satan Desired Worship in the Garden

Having failed at his attempt to receive worship by overthrowing the throne of God, Satan was cast to the earth along with a third of the angelic host who had joined him in his rebellion. "His tail drew a third of the stars of heaven and threw them to the earth" (Revelation 12:4). As a key part of God's "Grace Plan"[7] to resolve the angelic conflict, He created a new being called "man." Satan, still obsessed with receiving worship, attacked God by making a play for the worship of these newly created beings. He was not able to usurp God's authority, but perhaps he could usurp man's authority and take control of the earth, which God had given to man as his dominion. The issue as always is worship.

> There is no missing the parallel between Lucifer's "I will be like the Most High!" and the deceptive promise, "You will be like God." When Adam and Eve partook of the fruit, they "exchanged the truth of God for the lie, and worshipped and served the creature rather than the Creator" (Romans 1:25). Satan received the worship that he was seeking, and he is still receiving it wherever people substitute the creature for the Creator and believe the lie that they can be their own god.[8]

Throughout the biblical record, Satan has done everything he can to subvert the worship of God. He doesn't care what we worship as long as it is not God because as 1 Corinthians 10:14-22 teaches, when we bow down to anything, to any idol, we are, in fact, involved in demonic worship. "Rather, that the things which the Gentiles sacrifice they sacrifice to demons and not to God, and I do not want you to have fellowship with demons" (1 Corinthians 10:20). Anytime we fail to worship God, we are, by default, worshipping Satan.

Not only did Satan desire worship in heaven and in the Garden, but he also desired worship from Christ Jesus Himself.

Satan Desired Worship in the Desert

This is really quite incredible. Satan is so obsessed with receiving worship that he has the unmitigated gall to attempt to bribe the Son of God to give it to him. How desperate can he be? Here is Matthew's account of Satan's preposterous proposition:

> Again, the devil took Him up on an exceedingly high mountain, and showed Him all the kingdoms of the world and their glory. And he said to Him, "All these things I will give You if You will fall down and worship me." Then Jesus said to him, "Away with you, Satan! For it is written, *'You shall worship the LORD your God, and Him only you shall serve.'"* (Matthew 4:8-10, emphasis added)

Having been led by the Spirit into the wilderness after his baptism, Jesus comes face-to-face with the tempter who, true to form, begins his attack by twisting the Word of God and appealing to the flesh and the pride of life. Jesus deflected every "fiery dart of the wicked one" with "the shield of faith" and launched into His own offensive with His masterful use of "the sword of the Spirit, which is the word of God" (Ephesians 6:16-17). It is interesting to note that when Satan went toe-to-toe with Christ for the first time in Jesus' earthly ministry, the issue was worship. There is no mistaking that the prize being wrestled over here is who will receive worship.

Satan Will Desire Worship in the Temple during the Tribulation

After Satan's miserable failure to receive worship from Jesus during the wilderness temptation at the start of Christ's earthly ministry, and even after the crushing blow dealt Satan at the cross and the empty tomb, Satan refuses to accept his obvious defeat and continues to the very end seeking the worship he so desperately craves. The apostle Paul explains,

> Let no one deceive you by any means; for *that Day will not come* unless the falling away comes first, and the man of sin is revealed, the son of perdition, who opposes and exalts himself above all that is called God or that is worshipped, so that he sits as God in the temple of God, showing himself that he is God. (2 Thessalonians 2:3-4)

Jesus refers to this event in His Olivet Discourse concerning the signs before the end: "Therefore when you see the *'abomination of desolation,'* spoken of by Daniel the prophet, standing in the holy place (whoever reads, let him understand), then let those who are in Judea flee to the mountains" (Matthew 24:15-16).

After the rapture of the church, the "son of perdition"—the Antichrist—will come on the scene and unite the world under his authority. This is the beginning of the seven years of Tribulation. For three and one-half years, the world will be a utopia of peace and harmony as the Antichrist subtly wins the world over. This, however, is the proverbial "calm before the storm." At the midpoint of the Tribulation, the Antichrist, having deceived the Jews into accepting and supporting him, will enter the newly rebuilt temple in Jerusalem and set himself up as God.

> The Antichrist will cause a living statue of himself to be put into the temple, and his associate (the false prophet, Revelation 20:10) will cause the whole earth to worship it. Satan has always wanted the world's worship, and in the middle of the Tribulation he will begin to receive it (Matthew 4:8-11). Jesus called this statue "the abomination of desolation." (Daniel 9:27; Matthew 24:15)[9]

At this point, great tribulation beyond imagination will take place upon the earth. At the end of this seven-year period, the nations will gather at Armageddon to fight Israel and the Antichrist. But when they see the sign of Christ's coming they will join forces to fight Him. Jesus will defeat His enemies at this great battle, "and every eye will see Him, even they who pierced Him. And all the tribes of the earth will mourn because of Him" (Revelation 1:7). The Jews will at long last receive Christ as their Messiah, Satan will be bound, and Christ will set up His earthly kingdom and reign for one thousand years. At the end of that thousand-year reign, Satan will be released for a short time to gather up an army to fight against the saints one last time, at which time Christ will destroy the destroyer once and for all, and cast him into the lake of fire for ever. There will then be a new heaven and a new earth, "and there shall be no more curse, but the throne of God and of the Lamb shall be in it, and His servants shall serve [worship] Him" (Revelation 22:3).

The purpose of this section is not to go into a detailed explanation of the angelic conflict or the events of the end time, but simply to establish the fact that from the beginning of time the prize of spiritual warfare has always been worship. With an understanding of where the battle began and what the battle is about, we can better comprehend that the purpose of redemption is worship.

The Purpose of Redemption is Worship

Prophesied to Adam

Because Adam and Eve "exchanged the truth of God for the lie and worshipped and served the creature rather than the Creator" (Romans 1:25), man died spiritually as God said would happen. Man tried to cover his sin with fig leaves and learned that "human good" is not adequate to remove the stain of sin. With absolute horror, Adam and Eve watched for the first time the death of an innocent victim by which "God made tunics of skin, and clothed them" (Genesis 3:21) to cover their nakedness, for "without shedding of blood there is no remission [covering]" (Hebrews 9:22).

Because of Adam's sin, man lost his access to God. No longer could man walk with God in the cool of the day. No longer would he be able to worship God unhindered and uninhibited. Sin robbed man of his very reason for existence—to bring glory to God and to worship Him. "Behold, the LORD's hand is not shortened, that it cannot save; nor His ear heavy, that it cannot hear. But your iniquities have separated you from your God; and your sins have hidden *His* face from you, so that He will not hear" (Isaiah 59:1-2).

At once, "Operation Grace" was put into action. God in grace started the wheels of redemption rolling to reconcile helpless and hopeless man to Himself. "For by grace you have been saved through faith, and that not of yourselves; *it is* the gift of God, not of works, lest anyone should boast" (Ephesians 2:8-9). Here in the darkest hour of man's history, God offered a brilliant ray of light when he prophesied, "And I will put enmity between you [Satan] and the woman, and between your seed and her Seed; He [Christ] shall bruise your head, and you shall bruise His heel" (Genesis 3:15). Here is the first glorious prophecy concerning Christ's coming to purchase our redemption with His own blood upon the cross and removing the veil that separated us from being able to worship God in the very Holy of Holies—His very presence. Not only was redemption's purpose to restore worship seen in the *prophecy* to Adam, it was also seen in the *promise* to Abraham.

Promised to Abraham

Here is the biblical account of the promise:

> When Abram was ninety-nine years old, the LORD appeared to Abram and said to him, "I *am* Almighty God; walk before Me and be blameless. And I will make My covenant between Me and you, and will multiply you exceedingly." Then Abram fell on his face, and God talked with him, saying: "As for Me, behold, My covenant is with you, and you shall be a father of many nations. No longer shall your name be called Abram, but your name shall be Abraham; for I have made you a father of many nations … This *is* My covenant which you shall keep, between Me and you and your descendants after you: Every male child among you shall be circumcised. (Genesis 17:1-5, 10)

In this pivotal passage, God initiates a relationship with Abraham and makes a threefold covenant with him. In short, God promises Abraham much land, many descendants, and that the peoples of the earth would be blessed because of him. This was an obvious prophecy concerning Christ's redemption of mankind, as Matthew graphically points out in the first verse of the first book of the "new" covenant: "The book of the genealogy of Jesus Christ, the Son of David, the *Son of Abraham"* (Matthew 1:1, emphasis added). Matthew here wanted to remind us that Jesus' birth was the fulfillment of God's promise to Abraham.

This covenant between God and man—in this case, Abraham— as always, was sealed by blood. Circumcision was the sign that God introduced to seal this covenant relationship. Circumcision as it relates to redemption is also a symbol of restored worship. "Circumcision was meant to symbolize a commitment of oneself to God's will forever. It is an outward sign of a heart, the inner core of one's personality, dedicated to doing the will of God."[10]

Moses explained the spiritual meaning of circumcision. "And the LORD your God will circumcise your heart and the heart of your descendants, to love the LORD your God with all your heart and with all your soul, that you may live" (Deuteronomy 30:6). What an amazing verse linking the ritual of circumcision to worship and even more amazing to see the connection between ritual, in this case circumcision, and the idea of worship emanating from the heart.

Zwingli's influence on the Reformation has led many evangelicals to be skeptical of ritual and the use of symbols in worship. Zwingli believed that all the ceremonies, rituals, and traditions related to worship were in and of themselves paganistic. As a result, he determined to remove them all as much as possible from the corporate worship experience, with no regard as to whether or not they had any value.[11] This was an unfortunate overreaction to the excesses and abuses of these worship practices by the church in the late medieval period. The problem had become that instead of the ritual and the symbol directing attention to God in worship, it became an end to itself and took on an almost magical quality. If you said the right "magic" words or did the right "magic" things, God would be pleased and magically—hocus-pocus—you would receive what you desired. Worship then became simply a way to get what you wanted. By the way, the term "hocus-pocus" actually came from a misunderstanding of the Latin words said by the priest over the bread and wine that was supposed to change the elements into the actual body and blood of Christ.

I can't help but wonder if the current emphasis today in the church growth movement on using worship as a means to the end of attracting crowds is that far removed from the worship practices of the church prior to the Reformation when the church, in a misguided attempt to make its message attractive to the masses, attempted to incorporate many of the pagan celebrations and customs of the day into the church's worship practices. No doubt this was an effective means of "Christianizing" the various cultures, but it also had the negative effect of diluting the church's message by exposing it to the ungodly influence of the mystery cults and other pagan practices. I am concerned that the marketing mentality of increasing church attendance at all costs will dilute our message and bring us under the influence of humanistic pagan philosophies as well. The gospel, apart from the work of the Holy Spirit, will never be attractive to the unregenerate mind, as it will always be a "stumbling block" and will be considered foolish to a lost world. Paul explained that "we preach Christ crucified, to the Jews a stumbling block and to the Greeks foolishness" (1 Corinthians 1:23). In order to make the gospel palatable to the culture at large for the purpose of attracting the masses to our churches, we would have to water it down to the point of ineffectiveness.

My contention is that we do not have to "market" the gospel by "branding" our worship in such a way as to appeal to the unsaved. There has been created in the soul of man a God-shaped vacuum that is drawn to worship. Man is a worshipping creature. It has been proven in every culture around the world throughout time. Man, searching for an object of worship, will often settle for what is at hand if he has not been made aware of the claims of Christ upon his life. If a church will concentrate on worshipping God with the emphasis on pleasing Him and not on pleasing the masses, the result will be real church growth with depth as well as breadth. Jesus said, "And I, if I am lifted up from the earth, will draw all *peoples* to Myself" (John 12:32).

I am by no means against reaching the lost for Christ and growing churches (I have been blessed to have served in some of America's most evangelistic and fastest growing churches), but I would like to sound a word of caution that "we ought not allow worship to be accommodated to current cultural norms to such an extent that worship loses its meaning."[12] This is an excellent example of how a good understanding of worship history can help us not make the same mistake twice.

To continue our discussion of the importance of a right heart in worship, let's think about the message of the Old Testament prophets. You would think, at first glance, that they were opposed to the ritualistic temple sacrificial worship system, especially when you read passages like this one from the prophet Amos:

> [God said] I hate, I despise your feast days, and I do not savor your sacred assemblies. Though you offer Me burnt offerings and your grain offerings, I will not accept *them,* nor will I regard your fattened peace offerings. Take away from Me the noise of your songs, for I will not hear the melody of your stringed instruments. But let justice run down like water, and righteousness like a mighty stream. (Amos 5:21-24)

In spite of how that might sound, the prophets of old were not opposed to ritual and symbolism in worship. God had commanded them to do the ritual and to do it correctly, under severe penalty. The problem was that it was not done from the heart. "Inasmuch as these people draw near with their mouths and honor Me with their lips, but have removed their hearts far from Me" (Isaiah 29:13). Notice the similarity between

Deuteronomy 30:6 and Matthew 22:37-38 (a passage often used to teach the primacy of worship). "Jesus said to him, *'You shall love the LORD your God with all your heart, with all your soul, and with all your mind.'* This is *the* first and great commandment."

The point is that the use of symbols and ritual in worship is not the issue. Symbols and ritual were used in Old Testament worship and in the New. Worship is really impossible without them. If all you did in worship was preach the Word, you still cannot avoid the fact that words are themselves symbols that convey meaning. God has ordained that through certain symbols and by certain rituals the gospel is preached and understood, the most common being the Lord's Supper and believer's baptism. The issue then becomes one of the heart. The condition of the worshipper's heart is what makes the use of a symbol or a ritual true worship or false religion.

Paul links the concept of a circumcised heart directly to worship in his letter to the Philippians. "For we are the circumcision, who worship God in the Spirit, rejoice in Christ Jesus, and have no confidence in the flesh" (Philippians 3:3). Paul again speaks of circumcision of the heart in Romans 2:29, "But *he is* a Jew who *is one* inwardly; and circumcision *is that* of the heart, in the Spirit, not in the letter; whose praise *is* not from men but from God." The Scofield Reference Bible says of this verse,

> True Judaism was not merely a matter of external observances or precise keeping of ordinances but of a heart attitude toward God. As Paul says in v. 29, it is not in the letter but in the spirit. The Judaism that bases everything on minute and external observances (cp. Romans 2:28-29) is not true Judaism but a perversion, and was condemned by the Lord Jesus Christ. (Matthew 15:6)[13]

Philippians 3:3 and Romans 2:29 both emphasize having a circumcised heart *in the spirit,* which is reminiscent of Jesus' definitive teaching on worship in John 4 at Jacob's well. "God *is* Spirit, and those who worship Him must worship in spirit and truth" (John 4:24). In other words, to worship God *in spirit* is to worship Him with a circumcised heart. Circumcision was a symbol of the promise that God would restore us to our place as worshippers through the blood of Christ, and today, a Christian, living a lifestyle of worship is one who has a circumcised heart—a heart of purity and commitment to do the will of God in his life. Redemption's purpose in restoring worship can certainly be seen in the promise to Abraham.

Portrayed in the Exodus

Redemption's purpose in restoring worship is the central theme of the Exodus. When God commissioned Moses at the burning bush, Moses said to God, "Who am I, that I should go to Pharaoh and bring the Israelites out?" To which God replied, "I will be with you. And this will be the sign to you that it is I who have sent you: When you have brought the people out of Egypt, *you will worship God on this mountain*" (Exodus 3:11-12 NIV, emphasis added).

Later, on the way to Egypt,

> The LORD said to Moses, "When you return to Egypt, see that you perform before Pharaoh all the wonders I have given you the power to do. But I will harden his heart so that he will not let the people go. Then say to Pharaoh, 'This is what the Lord says: Israel is my firstborn son, and I told you, "Let my son go, *so he may worship me*." But you refused to let him go; so I will kill your firstborn son.'" (Exodus 4:21-23 NIV, emphasis added)

When Moses and Aaron stood before Pharaoh for the first time they demanded that they be set free to "hold a festival" to the Lord in the desert (Exodus 5:1). In Exodus 7:16, 8:1, 8:20, 9:1, 9:13, and 10:3, God makes it crystal clear to Pharaoh why He is demanding that the Hebrews be set free. "Let my people go so that they may worship me." David Peterson wrote, "The early chapters of Exodus suggest that a pilgrimage to meet God at 'the mountain of God' is the immediate focus of the narrative, and the liberation from slavery in Egypt was for the purpose of divine service of 'worship.'"[14]

Once Israel reached Sinai after their redemption from Egypt, Moses went up on the mountain to commune with God. There God instructed Moses what to tell the people about what it would mean to be in a covenant relationship with Him and just how His worship was to be accomplished. "Now if you obey me fully and keep my covenant, then out of all nations you will be my treasured possession. Although the whole earth is mine, you will be for me a kingdom of priests and a holy nation" (Exodus 19:5-6 NIV).

God redeemed them so that they might worship Him, and by this unique lifestyle of worship—obeying His Word and keeping His covenant—they would become a witness to the nations of the world to the wonderful grace of God. They would be the means by which God would keep His promise to Abraham that the nations of the world would be blessed through him (Genesis 12:2-3). Worship by its very nature is evangelistic.

Some have tried to set worship against evangelism in building contemporary churches. Yet the God-ordained method of world evangelism in the book of Exodus was worship. God Himself confirmed this to Pharaoh. "But indeed for this purpose I have raised you up, that I may show My power *in* you, and that My name may be declared in all the earth" (Exodus 9:16). Peter draws a tremendous analogy between Old Testament Israel and the New Testament Christian while commenting on this very issue, "But you *are* a chosen generation, a royal priesthood, a holy nation, His own special people, that you may proclaim the praises of Him who called you out of darkness into His marvelous light" (1 Peter 2:9).

This terminology is right out of Exodus 19:5-6: "Now therefore, if you will indeed obey My voice and keep My covenant, then you shall be *a special treasure* to Me above all people; for all the earth *is* Mine. And you shall be to Me *a kingdom of priests* and *a holy nation*" (emphasis added). As we live in a covenant relationship with God by a lifestyle of exclusive worship, we cannot help but be a witness to God's redeeming grace. Jesus' most comprehensive teaching on lifestyle worship in John 4 was crouched in a soul-winning experience. The Philippian jailer and his family were saved as a result of a midnight worship service conducted from a dungeon cell by Paul and Silas. When Peter and John appeared before Annas, the high priest, after their arrest, Peter, "filled with the Holy Spirit" witnessed to them of Christ, saying, "Nor is there salvation in any other, for there is no other name under heaven given among men by which we must be saved" (Acts 4:12).

It was obvious to those that heard Peter and John speak that their boldness and power was the result of their lifestyle of worship. "Now when they saw the boldness of Peter and John, and perceived that they were uneducated and untrained men, they marveled. And they realized that *they had been with Jesus*" (Acts 4:13, emphasis added). When you have been with Jesus in worship, you will say like Peter and John, "For we cannot but speak the things which we have seen and heard" (Acts 4:20). Worship is not the antithesis of evangelism; it is its very essence.

> The history of the church is the story of believing people storming the gates of hell and delivering those held in sin's bondage. The military images used of the church in the New Testament ought to convince us that the Christian life is more than joyful fellowship or quiet meditation. It is a battle that we cannot escape and that we dare not lose; and the key to our victory is worship.[15]

There can be no worship apart from redemption. John tells us that the purpose of evangelism is to redeem worshippers for God's glory.

> Then I saw another angel flying in the midst of heaven, having the everlasting gospel to preach to those who dwell on the earth—to every nation, tribe, tongue, and people—saying with a loud voice, "Fear God and give glory to Him, for the hour of His judgment has come; and worship Him who made heaven and earth, the sea and springs of water." (Revelation 14:6-7)

Worship for the Israelite was a celebration of the Exodus event. Worship for the Christian is a celebration of the Christ event. Both events were centered in redemption, the former a foreshadowing of the latter. Redemption's purpose in restoring worship was graphically portrayed in the Exodus.

Provided by Christ

Prophesied to Adam, promised to Abraham, and portrayed in the Exodus is the fact that our ability to worship God is a result of God's redemptive plan of grace provided by Christ. He is the focal point—the apex—the culmination—of God's program to restore worshippers to their original place of service before Him. Gabriel announced the good news to Joseph that Mary would have a son. Gabriel instructed Joseph that they were to call him Jesus, which means Savior, "for He will save His people from their sins" (Matthew 1:21). Jesus was born to save, He lived to save, He died to save, and "therefore He is also able to save to the uttermost those who come to God through Him, since He always lives to make intercession for them" (Hebrews 7:25).

Jesus came to save us from the sin that prevents us from approaching a holy God in worship. Sin is to worship what matter is to anti-matter—they are diametrically opposed to one another; they cannot co-exist in the same time and space. Sin annihilated worship when Satan refused to honor God in heaven. Sin abolished worship when man refused to believe God in the Garden. Sin abrogated worship when Abraham refused to believe God in the matter concerning Hagar. Sin annulled worship when the Israelites refused to believe God at the incident of the golden calf. Sin is the barrier that denies us access to a holy God.

As I have already mentioned in our discussion of tabernacle worship in Chapter 5, we cannot help but be impressed with the numerous barriers that kept the would-be worshipper out of the Holy of Holies. The architectural design of the tabernacle emphasized man's sin and unworthiness to stand before God. Because God is holy and man is unholy, we have been alienated from Him since Eden. "Therefore, just as through one man [Adam] sin entered the world, and death through sin, and thus death spread to all men, because all sinned" (Romans 5:12). The Greek word translated "death" is *thanatos*. Zodhiates comments on this word, "As spiritual life consists in constant communication with God who is life, so spiritual death is the separation from His blessed influence."[16]

In the Garden of Eden, man enjoyed constant fellowship with his God. But because of sin, he lost that privilege and was cast out of the Garden and excommunicated from the presence of God. God's promise to Adam and Abraham, the tabernacle with its altars and sacrifices, and the entire system of worship instituted at Sinai was all in hope that the blessed one was coming "in the name of the Lord" (Psalm 118:26) by whom "we have been sanctified through the offering of the body of Jesus Christ once *for all*" (Hebrews 10:10).

So, by the grace of God, in the fullness of time, on a windswept hill, from a rugged Roman cross, there echoed down through the dungeons of hell, across the sea of time, into the eons of eternity, the long-awaited victory cry from parched and precious lips, "Tetelestai! It is finished!" Redemption's work is done! The final price for sin has been paid in full. It is finished, Adam! Your promised seed has crushed the serpent's head. It is finished, Abraham! God indeed has provided Himself a Lamb for the sacrifice. It is finished, Moses! At long last we boldly enter the Holy of Holies to worship God beyond the veil.

> Therefore, brethren, having boldness to enter the Holiest by the blood of Jesus, by a new and living way which He consecrated for us, through the veil, that is, His flesh, and *having* a High Priest over the house of God, let us draw near with a true heart in full assurance of faith. (Hebrews 10:19-22)

Notice that blessed invitation "let us draw near." A man does not draw near to God except to worship Him. For centuries, our sin has prevented us from approaching a thrice-holy God in worship. But now, because of the blood of Jesus, we have been redeemed—redeemed that we might draw near in restored relationship with a true heart and, like Adam and Eve before the Fall, walk with Him in the cool of the day, and to worship Him unashamed and uninhibited. Hallelujah! Redemption's purpose in restoring us to a lifestyle of worship has been provided by Christ.

Proclaimed in Eternity

In the Revelation, worship and redemption are heard wafting around the throne of God like two intertwining themes played in majestic counterpoint.

> And they sang a new song, saying: "You are worthy to take the scroll, and to open its seals; for You were slain, and have redeemed us to God by Your blood out of every tribe and tongue and people and nation, and have made us kings and priests to our God; and we shall reign on the earth … Worthy is the Lamb who was slain to receive power and riches and wisdom, and strength and honor and glory and blessing!" And every creature which is in heaven and on the earth and under the earth and such as are in the sea, and all that are in them, I heard saying:
>
> "Blessing and honor and glory and power *be* to Him who sits on the throne,
>
> And to the Lamb, forever and ever!"

> Then the four living creatures said, "Amen!" And the twenty-four elders fell down and worshiped Him who lives forever and ever. (Revelation 5:9-10, 12-14)

To understand the book of Revelation is to understand that the one occupation that will consume us for all eternity is worship. In fact, the worship and praise that will take place around God's throne at the marriage supper of the Lamb will be the fulfillment and culmination of all the events put into motion after Satan's rebellion to redeem man and restore him to his place of communion and fellowship with his Creator. In Isaiah 25:6-8, we see Israel's longing to someday sit at a feast with their God where "He will swallow up death forever, and the Lord GOD will wipe away tears from all faces; the rebuke of His people He will take away from all the earth" (Isaiah 25:8). At long last that longing will be satisfied, as described by John the Revelator:

> They shall neither hunger anymore nor thirst anymore; the sun shall not strike them, nor any heat; for the Lamb who is in the midst of the throne will shepherd them and lead them to living fountains of waters. And God will wipe away every tear from their eyes. (Revelation 7:16-17)

The phrase, "and lead them to living [springing] fountains of water" could be a reference to Jesus' discussion with the woman at the well, when He said, "Whoever drinks of this water will thirst again, but whoever drinks of the water that I shall give him will never thirst. But the water that I shall give him will become in him a fountain of water springing up into everlasting life" (John 4:13-14).

Jesus is obviously the "Lamb" mentioned in Revelation 7:17 who is providing the same "living fountains of water" that He also offered to the Samaritan woman. Isaiah even tells us what these waters symbolize. "Therefore with joy you will draw water from the wells of salvation" (Isaiah 12:3). The "living water" is the water of salvation, and by inference, the Lord Himself because He is its source. Jeremiah writes, "For My people have committed two evils: they have forsaken Me, the fountain of living waters, *and* hewn themselves cisterns—broken cisterns that can hold no water" (Jeremiah 2:13).

Israel had forsaken the worship of God that would have refreshed and sustained them like a gushing fountain for the stagnant, stale worship of the gods of this world. But in God's grace and mercy, "the rebuke of his people shall he take away" (Isaiah 25:8), and we together will sing with the millions around the throne for all eternity.

> After these things I heard a loud voice of a great multitude in heaven, saying, "Alleluia! Salvation and glory and honor and power *belong* to the Lord our God! … And I heard, as it were, the voice of a great multitude, as the sound of many waters and as the sound of mighty thunderings, saying, "Alleluia! For the Lord God Omnipotent reigns! Let us be glad and rejoice and give Him glory, for the marriage of the Lamb has come, and His wife has made herself ready." And to her it was granted to be arrayed in fine linen, clean and bright, for the fine linen is the righteous acts of the saints. (Revelation 19:1, 6-8)

Our ability to participate in this eternal worship service was made possible by the blood of the Lamb that wrapped us in robes of righteousness both "clean and bright." As states the majestic hymn:

> When He shall come with trumpet sound,
> Oh, may I then in Him be found;
> Dressed in His righteousness alone,
> Faultless to stand before the throne.[17]

Redemption's purpose in restoring us to our ordained occupation as worshippers of the mighty God was *prophesied* to Adam, *promised* to Abraham, *portrayed* in the Exodus, *provided* by Christ, and will be *proclaimed* throughout all eternity.

Realizing that the *prize* of spiritual warfare is worship, and that the *purpose* of redemption is worship, we can now understand that …

The Process of Discipleship is Worship

The Assignment—Make Disciples

Before Jesus' ascension, He asked His disciples to meet Him at a particular place. "Then the eleven disciples went away into Galilee, to the mountain which Jesus had appointed for them. When they saw Him, *they worshipped Him*" (Matthew 28:16-17, emphasis added). Jesus, reminiscent of Daniel's prophecy in Daniel 7:13-14, emphasized His authority and then gave them the following assignment:

> Go therefore and make disciples of all the nations, baptizing them in the name of the Father and of the Son and of the Holy Spirit, teaching them to observe all things that I have commanded you; and lo, I am with you always, *even* to the end of the age. Amen. (Matthew 28:19-20)

It is important to note the close proximity of the disciple's *worship* in verse seventeen, and the disciple's *work* that was assigned to them in verses nineteen and twenty. The work assignment was given in the context of an intimate worship time with Jesus. Our work for God always proceeds from our worship of God—never the other way around. Warren Wiersbe wrote,

> Evangelism divorced from true worship can become merely a program tacked on to an already overloaded ecclesiastical machine, or, even worse, a struggle for statistics and "results." Isaiah became an evangelist *after* attending a worship service in the temple and seeing God "high and lifted up" (Isaiah 6:1). Evangelism is an essential part of the church's ministry, but it must be the result of worship, or it will not glorify God.[18]

In the Matthew 28:19-20 passage, the Greek word translated "teach" is *matheteuo*, which means "disciple."

> *Matheteuo* must be distinguished from the verb *matheo* (which is not found in the NT), which simply means to learn without any attachment to the teacher who teaches. *Matheteuo* means not only to learn but to become attached to one's teacher and to become his follower in doctrine and conduct. It is really not sufficient to translate this verb "learn" but as "making a disciple."[19]

So the assignment we have been given is to "make disciples." What exactly does that mean?

The Aim—To be Like Christ

By definition a disciple is one who attaches himself to his teacher and begins to do what he does. If that is so, then the aim of discipleship for the Christian is to be like Christ. Paul wrote that God's ultimate purpose for us is *"to be* conformed to the image of His Son" (Romans 8:29). What, then, is the definitive quality that best sums up the character of Christ that we

90

should emulate? I would submit that it is the quality of worship. David Peterson said, "Jesus offers the perfect pattern or model of acceptable worship in his obedient lifestyle."[20]

I have heard it said that Jesus did not teach much about worship, so it must not be very important. I think that mind-set trivializes Jesus' emphasis on worship in His encounter with Satan in the wilderness and in His discourse with the Samaritan woman at the well. Even then, Jesus did not need to say anything specific about worship; He was worship personified! If we want to know how to live a lifestyle of worship, we should find ourselves "looking unto Jesus, the author and finisher of *our* faith" (Hebrews 12:2). Jesus was the essence and epitome of what a worshipper of God should be, so to truly be a disciple of Christ in the sense of *matheteuo* would require us to be worshippers as well. The *assignment* is to make disciples. The *aim* is to be like Christ. The *approach* is to cultivate a lifestyle of worship.

The Approach—Lifestyle Worship

Worship is the biblical means by which we become more like Christ. Paul wrote to the church at Corinth, "And we, who with unveiled faces all reflect [contemplate] the Lord's glory, are being transformed into his likeness with ever-increasing glory, which comes from the Lord, who is the Spirit" (2 Corinthians 3:18 NIV).

You will recall that after Moses had come from worshipping in the presence of the Lord on Mount Sinai, his face glowed with God's glory, so much so that the people were afraid to approach him until he covered his face with a veil. Paul compares Moses' veil to the veil over the hearts and minds of the Jews who are still operating under the law. This veil can only be removed when an individual accepts Christ as his Savior and Lord, which is accomplished by the power of the Spirit. He then likens the freedom that results from the presence of the Spirit to the freedom the Israelites experienced when they were released from Egyptian bondage. "Now the Lord is the Spirit, and where the Spirit of the Lord is, there is freedom" (2 Corinthians 3:17 NIV). A person who has accepted Christ is no longer in bondage to the law. The veil over that person's mind and heart is lifted at conversion, so that he now has the freedom to reflect or contemplate God's glory.

To reflect or contemplate God's glory is to worship God in the context of His Word. The NIV translates the Greek word *katoptrizomai* as "reflect" or "contemplate." The KJV translates it as "beholding as in a glass." The NASB translates it "beholding as in a mirror." James tells us the Word of God is like a mirror (James 1:22-25). He illustrates this truth by comparing a man who reads the Word of God and makes no adjustment in his life to a man who looks in a mirror and makes no adjustment in his appearance. The inference is, what is the point of looking in the mirror if you plan to make no changes? James writes, "But the man who looks intently into the perfect law that gives freedom, and continues to do this, not forgetting what he has heard, but doing it—he will be blessed in all he does" (James 1:25 NIV).

One of my dad's early heroes in the ministry was the black preacher Manuel Scott. After hearing Dr. Scott preach one evening my dad had the opportunity to have breakfast with him the next day. As a young preacher, my dad expressed to Dr. Scott how much he was blessed, encouraged and inspired by his preaching and the truths he was able to extrapolate out of the Scripture. My dad said, "Dr. Scott it is so evident that you are a spiritual man. How can I learn to preach with the insights and depth with which you preach? How does a man become spiritual?" Manuel Scott thought for a moment and said, "Well, Harold, when you wake up in the morning start your day by reading and studying the Word of God, and then throughout the day continue to think about and meditate on what you've read. And then as you pillow your head in the evening, allow your heart and mind to be sanctified and cleansed "with the washing of water by the Word" (Ephesians 5:26)." Then Dr. Scott paused and reached up to put his thumbs under his red suspenders and with a smile said, "If you'll do that, Harold, then one of these days, you'll just wake up … spiritual!"

A man who is worshipping God in the context of His Word—reflecting and contemplating His glory—will be "transformed into the same image from glory to glory" (2 Corinthians 3:18). "The idea of transformation refers to an invisible process in Christians which takes place or begins to take place already during their life in this age."[21] Warren Wiersbe explains,

> As we worship Him and behold His glory, we are transformed by His Spirit to share in His own image and glory. Instead of

hiding a fading glory [like Moses did], we reveal an increasing glory that causes others to see Christ and honor Him.[22]

Paul also makes the connection between worship and discipleship in his address to Felix. "But this I confess to you, that according to the Way which they call a sect, so I worship [*latreuo*] the God of my fathers, believing all things which are written in the Law and in the Prophets" (Acts 24:14). Paul describes his lifestyle and ministry as a way to worship and serve the Lord, indicated in the use of the word *latreuo*, which means "to serve; in a religious sense to worship God."[23] Paul also indicates in this verse that this lifestyle of worship accomplished by "following the Way," or being a disciple of Christ, fulfills the law and the prophets. Worship and discipleship are inextricably interrelated.

John described this correlation between worship and discipleship when he said, "Beloved, now we are children of God; and it has not yet been revealed what we shall be, but we know that when He is revealed, *we shall be like Him, for we shall see Him as He is*" (1 John 3:2, emphasis added). The psalmist, referring to those who worship idols wrote, "Those who make them are like them; *so is* everyone who trusts in them" (Psalm 115:8). We do indeed become like what we worship.

Romans 12:1-2 teaches us clearly that worship is the means by which the Christian is transformed into the image of Christ. Albert W. Palmer said this about worship's ability to transform,

> [To worship God] means a release of energy. It puts into life something that steps it up to a higher voltage. Through worship, man comes to God at firsthand, has an immediate experience with God, and goes forth transformed and stimulated to new levels of endeavor.[24]

We are "discipled" as we behold His face in worship. "The goal of worship is Christlikeness in our character and conduct ... God's call to true worship, to an experience of transformation, is a call to dangerous and costly Christian living."[25]

Genuine worship is transforming—it is life changing. No one who has been in the presence of God ever goes away the same. I know I'm spiritualizing this, but I can't help but think about what Scripture says concerning the three wise men who after they had given their offerings of worship to the Christ child there at Bethlehem went home "a different way" (Matthew 2:12 NCV). Anyone who has looked on the face of the King of Kings and Lord of Lords in a genuine worship experience will, like the Magi, go away transformed, changed forever, never to be the same again. Genuine worship is indeed the biblical means by which we become more like Christ.

Conclusion

I have endeavored to show that the *prize* of spiritual warfare is worship, the *purpose* of redemption is worship, and the *process* of discipleship is worship. Spiritual warfare, redemption, and discipleship are all different facets of the concept called "lifestyle worship."

Living a lifestyle of worship involves a simple principal.

Lifestyle worship boiled down to its basic essence is the attitude that every situation of life is a call to worship. Our spiritual maturity is not measured by how we worship God when all is well, but rather how we worship Him down in the nitty-gritty of life when nothing seems to go right, when we are inundated with aggravations and distractions, and when we have been offended or hurt by others. When Satan tested Job, Job lost everything he had—his children, his wealth, and his health. In fact, his wife's advice to him was to "curse God and die" (Job 2:9). But in spite of all that, Job exclaimed, "Though He slay me, yet will I trust Him" (Job 13:15). Several verses come to mind as I think about this truth: "Every situation of life is a call to worship."

Paul wrote to the church at Thessalonica, "In *everything* give thanks; for this is the will of God in Christ Jesus for you" (1 Thessalonians 5:18, emphasis added). Do you remember what Job said? "Though He slay me, yet will I *trust* Him" (Job 13:15, emphasis added). The issue here is one of trust. Every situation of life can be a call to worship when we learn to trust God. We demonstrate our trust in God by giving thanks in everything that happens with the understanding that this is God's will for us. Your life is not at the mercy of fate and circumstance, floating like a cork bobber on a boisterous sea with no aim or direction. You are not being tossed around helplessly out of control by the winds of uncertainty. God has a plan for you, and that plan is to make you more like Christ—to conform you into His image. Paul wrote, "And we know that all things work together for good to those who love God, to those who are the called according to *His* purpose. For whom He foreknew, He also predestined *to be* conformed to the image of His Son" (Romans 8:28-29).

We can thank God in everything and worship Him in the darkest moments because all things work together for our good and God's glory. The "good" that is mentioned in Romans 8:28 is spelled out specifically in verse 29. Our circumstances—the good, the bad, and the ugly—are designed by God to press us into the image of Christ. God didn't save us to make us happy; he saved us to make us holy. "For it is God who works in you both to will and to do for *His* good pleasure" (Philippians 2:13, emphasis added).

We were not created for our pleasure; we were created for God's pleasure. We were created to worship Him. Don't get me wrong, Jesus did come to give us abundant life (John 10:10), but we will never be happy trying to be happy. That puts the emphasis on us. We were designed by God to worship *Him*. We will only find fulfillment and purpose in our lives as we live for the purpose for which we were created. When the emphasis of our lives is on *our* happiness, we begin to ride an emotional roller coaster that goes up and down with the circumstances of life. But when we place our emphasis on worshipping God and becoming more like Jesus, we can thank God in everything that happens; trusting Him that these events will make us more like Christ, which will bring glory to God, which is why we were created, and which will give us the greatest sense of satisfaction and purpose in our life.

Living a lifestyle of worship requires a simple plan.

Let me suggest a simple two-step plan that will transform the way you think about your circumstances and will help you learn to live your life from moment-to-moment as an offering of worship before God.

Step One: There must be an honest evaluation.

We must honestly identify every situation that we find ourselves in right now that makes us angry, bitter, depressed, or offended for our self, a family member, or a friend. If those emotions are present, obviously we aren't thanking God for the situation that He has allowed in our lives to make us more like Christ. At this point, we are actually resisting His attempts to make us holy. This is clearly disobedience to I Thessalonians 5:18, "In everything give thanks; for this is the will of God in Christ Jesus for you."

The Bible word for disobedience is *sin*. Remember, sin and worship cannot coexist. Sin must be confessed if we want a right relationship with God. First John 1:9 says, "If we confess our sins, He is faithful and just to forgive us *our* sins and to cleanse us from all unrighteousness." There is no need to live in disobedience and sin a second longer. Paul implored the believers at Corinth, "Therefore, having these promises, beloved, let us cleanse ourselves from all filthiness of the flesh and spirit, perfecting holiness in the fear of God" (2 Corinthians 7:1). Someone has wisely observed that a person's spiritual maturity can be measured by how long he will go with unconfessed sin in his heart.

Step Two: There must be a grateful realization.

We need to begin now to recognize that every situation of life is a call to worship. We should thank God for every hurt, disappointment, and aggravation that may come our way and allow them to bring us to Him in worship as we express our trust in Him. The result will be God's glory and our enjoying the "peace of God, which surpasses all understanding" (Philippians 4:7).

In Ephesians 5:18-20, Paul describes so well a person living a lifestyle of worship who has made the grateful realization that every situation of life is a call to worship.

> And do not be drunk with wine, in which is dissipation; but be filled with the Spirit, speaking to one another in psalms and hymns and spiritual songs, singing and making melody in your heart to the Lord, *giving thanks always for all things* to God the Father in the name of our Lord Jesus Christ. (Ephesians 5:18-20, emphasis added)

Notice that "giving thanks for all things" follows "speaking to one another in psalms and hymns and spiritual songs, singing and making melody in your heart to the Lord." When we begin to praise God and worship Him for who He is and what He has done, we realize that he is able to do "exceedingly abundantly above all that we ask or think, according to the power that works in us" (Ephesians 3:20). God's power is working in us through the difficulties of life, and as we worship Him with grateful hearts, our faith is strengthened and sustained.

My challenge to you today is simply this. If you really desire to live a lifestyle of worship before God, learn to make every situation of life a call to worship. Your response to the difficulties of life will reveal whether you are a worshipper of self or a worshipper of God. That is the essence of what it means to live before God in a lifestyle of worship.

Chapter 9

The Invitation

By becoming the Bridegroom to the church,
Christ Jesus has brought a sweet, glorious
intimacy back to the believers, so that we can
have a need-meeting relationship with Him.

—Judson Cornwall

During the course of this discussion, I have sought to introduce the study of worship by showing that we have been *created* to worship, that we have been *commanded* to worship, and that we have been *called* to worship.

We have discussed the importance of a right theology of worship—a theology that is *balanced* between spirit and truth, *basic* to our understanding of God's purpose in our redemption, and *biblical* if it is to be acceptable to God.

We have examined a proper understanding of worship history that is *foundational* to our being able to build on our past, *educational* in comprehending our present practices, and *interrelational* in helping us to appreciate our past common worship roots and the future convergence of our worship theologies when we, with glorified understanding, worship God in one accord for all eternity around His throne.

We have peered into the Old Testament tabernacle to see illustrated for us God's plan for redemption in Christ, who at once was the Great High Priest and God's sacrificial Lamb and who by rending the veil of His sinless body gave us access to the Holy of Holies and restored us to the purpose for which we had been created—the worship of God. Everything we lost because of Adam—our access to God, our knowledge of God, and our eternal life—was restored to us because of Christ and His finished work on the cross. He is the *way* back to God. He is the *truth* of who God is. He is the *life*—eternal, everlasting, and abundant.

We have considered the use of praise in our worship: its *power,* its *pattern,* its *people,* and the *person* to whom it should be directed. We have analyzed the ministry of the worship leader as demonstrated in the life of John the Baptist, whose ministry was *preceded by a call, public in its character,* and *pure in its conduct.* We have discovered that in order to live a lifestyle of worship we must understand that the *prize* of spiritual warfare is worship, the *purpose* of redemption is worship, and the *process* by which we are discipled is worship. We have learned that every situation of life is a call to worship.

This has been an exciting journey as we have analyzed and scrutinized this wonderful doctrine of worship, but we must be careful that we do not become so technical and academic that we forget that worship is above all a personal relationship with God, in Christ, by the Spirit. With that caution in mind, consider with me for a moment God's invitation to you and me.

"So the King will greatly desire your beauty; because He *is* your Lord, worship Him" (Psalm 45:11). The Moffatt translation reads like this, "And when the king desires your beauty, yield to him—He is your Lord." Psalm 27:4 says, "One *thing* I have desired of the LORD, that will I seek: that I may dwell in the house of the LORD all the days of my life, to behold the beauty of the LORD, and to inquire in His temple." It would be reasonable that we would desire our Lord's beauty, but look again at Psalm 45:11, "So the King will greatly desire *your* beauty" (emphasis added). What an awesome thought that God finds us beautiful and desires intimacy with us. The apostle Paul wrote,

> For I am persuaded that neither death nor life, nor angels nor principalities nor powers, nor things present nor things to come, nor height nor depth, nor any other created thing, shall be able to separate us from the love of God which is in Christ Jesus our Lord. (Romans 8:38-39)

Jesus truly is the lover of our souls. We love Him because He first loved us. We did not seek Him; He sought us. Jesus, the magnificent Bridegroom, has showered His love and affection on his tender bride—on His church—on you and me.

As a young man and a young woman hopelessly in love shut out the world as they gaze into each other's eyes, so we, enraptured by the Savior's love, turn our eyes upon Jesus and find "that the things of earth grow strangely dim in the light of his glory and grace."[1] We can see His overtures of love all around us as He woos us to Himself. We have been "accepted in the Beloved" (Ephesians 1:6). We are beautiful in His eyes. How could we resist a lover like this—this lover of our souls?

There is nothing more beautiful to a groom than his bride. There is nothing he desires more than to spend precious time with her. His love for her is so great, so compelling, that he would give his very life to prove his love for her. "But God demonstrates His own love toward us, in that while we were still sinners, Christ died for us" (Romans 5:8). His love for us is beyond our comprehension and ability to understand. Don't resist his overtures of affection. Submit to Him. He so desires communion with you. Bathe your heart in His letters of love—His precious Word. Share with Him your deepest desires and most tender thoughts as you speak to Him in prayer. Don't become so preoccupied with life that you miss His still small voice calling you to love and worship.

Life's darkest moments are no match for the light of His love. The Apostle Paul wrote, "For I consider that the sufferings of this present time are not worthy *to be compared* with the glory which shall be revealed in us" (Romans 8:18). As you spend time with the Lover of your soul, your love for Him will deepen and broaden, and you will find that you will become more and more like Him. Godliness and holiness are not accomplished by great effort, but they are a natural expression of a love relationship with our beautiful Bridegroom—the Lord Jesus. Hear the King's invitation today. Respond in worship. "So the King will greatly desire your beauty; because He *is* your Lord, worship Him" (Psalm 45:11)."[2]

Notes

Preface

1. Robert E. Webber, "Preparations for Becoming a Worship Leader," *Worship Leader Magazine* 1 (February/ March 1992), 10.

Chapter 2—Worship's Purpose: Introduction to Worship

1. Spiros Zodhiates, ed., *The Complete Word Study Old Testament* (Chattanooga: AMG Publishers, 1994), s.v. "Tselem," 2358.
2. H.D.M. Spence and Joseph S. Exell, eds., *The Pulpit Commentary* (Grand Rapids: William B. Eerdmans Publishing Company, 1950), vol. 1: *Genesis,* 54-55.
3. Spiros Zodhiates, ed., *The Complete Word Study New Testament* (Chattanooga: AMG Publishers, 1991), s.v. "Metamorphoo," 1111.
4. Ibid., s.v. "Eikon," 909.
5. Ibid., s.v. "Agapao," 878.
6. Webster's Seventh New Collegiate Dictionary (Springfield: G. & C. Merriam Company, Publishers, 1965), s.v. "Worship."
7. Cf. Matthew 22:35-40. Matthew Henry, *Commentary on the Whole Bible*, ed. Leslie F. Church (Grand Rapids: Zondervan Publishing Company, 1960), 1318.
8. Robert E. Webber, *Worship Is a Verb* (Peabody: Hendrickson Publishers, Inc., 2004).
9. Ben Patterson, *The Grand Essentials* (Waco: Word Books, 1987), 46-47.

Chapter 3—Worship's Procedure: Theology of Christian Worship

1. Roger Spradlin, "Imitating the Incarnation," sermon preached at Valley Baptist Church, 7 August 1994 (Bakersfield: Valley Baptist Church Tape Ministry).
2. Warren W. Wiersbe, *Real Worship It Will Transform Your Life* (Nashville: Thomas Nelson Publishers, 1986), 24.
3. Aiden Wilson Tozer. AZQuotes.com, Wind and Fly LTD, 2015. http://www.azquotes.com/quote/933337, accessed December 15, 2015.
4. Jack W. Hayford, *Worship His Majesty* (Dallas: Word Publishing, 1987), 77.
5. Robert E. Webber, *Worship Old and New* (Grand Rapids: Zondervan Publishing House, 1982), 35-36.
6. David Peterson, *Engaging With God: A Biblical Theology of Worship* (Grand Rapids: William B. Eerdmans Publishing Company, 1992), 20.

Chapter 4—Worship's Past: History of Christian Worship

1. A. W. Tozer, *Whatever Happened To Worship* (Camp Hill: Christian Publication, 1985), 49-50.
2. Robert E. Webber, *Worship Old and New* (Grand Rapids: Zondervan Publishing House, 1982), 12.
3. Ibid.
4. Ibid., 14-15.
5. Ibid., 15.
6. Ibid.
7. James F. White, *Introduction to Christian Worship* (Nashville: Abingdon Press, 1993), 11.

Chapter 5—Worship's Pattern: Tabernacle Worship

1. Walter B. Knight, *Knight's Master Book of New Illustrations* (Grand Rapids: William B. Eerdmans Publishing Co., 1956), 326-327.

2.   Charles Wesley, "'Tis Finished! The Messiah Dies." *The Baptist Hymnal*, Wesley L. Forbis, ed. (Nashville: Convention Press, 1991), 148.

Chapter 6—Worship's Power: Praise and Worship

1.   James Draper, *More Than a Song* (Chicago: Moody Monthly, 1970), 3.
2.   Adapted from Jack Hyles, "The Real Need of Evangelistic Music," in *How to Build an Evangelistic Music Program,* by Lindsey Terry (Nashville: Thomas Nelson Publishers, 1974), 19-20.
3.   Adapted from Robert G. Lee, *Latest of Lee* (Jefferson City: Le Roi Publishers, 1973), 32-33.
4.   Original author unknown. Adapted and compiled from *God With Us: A Worship Experience for all Seasons* (Mobile: Integrity Music, Inc., 1993), 142-143; from Robert J. Wells, *Prophetic Messages for Modern Times* (Dallas: Texas Printing House, Inc., 1944), 205-206, and numerous versions from various online sources.

Chapter 7—Worship's Practice: The Heart of the Worship Leader

1.   Ron Dunn, quoted in Don McMinn, *A Heart Aflame!* (Oklahoma City: NCM Press, 1993), 27.
2.   Merrill C. Tenney. *Handy Dictionary of the Bible* (Grand Rapids: Zondervan, 1965), s.v. "Prophecy, Prophets."
3.   A. A. MacRae. "Prophets and Prophecy," in *The Zondervan Pictorial Encyclopedia of the Bible,* Merrill C. Tenney and Steven Barabas, eds. (Grand Rapids: Zondervan Publishing House, 1976), Vol. 4, 875.
4.   Zodhiates, *The Complete Word Study New Testament,* s.v. "Oikodome," 940.
5.   Ibid., s.v. "Paraklesis," 944.
6.   Ibid., s.v. "Parakletos," 944.
7.   W. E. Vine, *The Expanded Vine's Expository Dictionary of New Testament Words,* ed. John Kohlenberger (Minneapolis: Bethany House, 1984), s.v. "Comfort, Comforter, Comfortless," 199.

8. Zodhiates, *The Complete Word Study New Testament,* s.v. "Aggelos," 878.

9. Tenney, *Handy Dictionary of the Bible*, s.v. "Kingdom of God."

10. Henry, *Commentary on the Whole Bible*, 1364.

11. Inspired by a quote from Warren W. Wiersbe, *The Bible Exposition Commentary* (Wheaton: Victor Books, 1989), Vol. 1, 287.

12. See Matthew 4:23, 9:35, 24:14, Mark. 1:14.

13. Webber, *Worship Is a Verb*, 45.

14. Henry, *Commentary on the Whole Bible*, 1409.

15. Vine, *The Expanded Vine's Expository Dictionary of New Testament Words,* s.v. "Yield."

16. *Webster's Seventh New Collegiate Dictionary,* 1965 ed., s.v. "Yield".

17. Watchman Nee, quoted in McMinn, *A Heart Aflame!,* 39.

18. Sally Kock, cited in "Quotable Quotes," *Readers Digest,* January 1994, 119.

19. Zodhiates, *The Complete Word Study New Testament,* s.v. "Paraginomai."

20. G. Giacumakis, Jr., "Desert," in *The Zondervan Pictorial Encyclopedia of the Bible,* vol. 2, 106.

21. Vance Havner, *The Vance Havner Quote Book,* Dennis J. Hester compiler (Grand Rapids: Baker Book House, 1986), 65.

22. Havner, *The Vance Havner Quote Book,* 166.

23. J. Oswald Sanders, *Spiritual Leadership* (Chicago: Moody Press, 1967), 73.

24. M. R. DeHaan and Henry G. Bosch, eds., *Bread for Each Day* (Grand Rapids: Zondervan, 1962), July 10.

25. Spence, *The Pulpit Commentary,* vol. 15: *Matthew,* 77.

26. *Webster's Seventh New Collegiate Dictionary,* s.v. "Personality."

27. W. C. Kaiser, "Name," in *The Zondervan Pictorial Encyclopedia of the Bible,* Vol.4, 363.

28. Ibid.

29. Roswell C. Long, quoted in Frank S. Mead, editor and compiler, *12,000 Religious Quotations* (Grand Rapids: Baker Book House, 1989), s.v. "Worship."

30. H. L. Willmington, *Willmington's Guide to the Bible* (Wheaton: Tyndale House, 1981), 483-484.

31. Tenney, *Handy Dictionary of the Bible,* s.v. "Nazarite."

32. Jerry Bridges, *The Pursuit of Holiness* (Colorado Springs: NavPress, 1978), 19.

33. D. J. Fant, *A. W. Tozer,* 73, 83; quoted in Sanders, *Spiritual Leadership,* 74.

34. Spence, *The Pulpit Commentary,* Vol. 16: *Mark,* 2.

35. Havner, *The Vance Havner Quote Book,* 11.

36. George Whitefield, quoted in John Blanchard, *Gathered Gold* (Welwyn, England: Evangelical Press, 1984), 155.

37. S. L. Brengle, *The Soulwinner's Secret,* quoted in Sanders, *Spiritual Leadership,* 18.

Chapter 8—Worship's Priority: Lifestyle Worship

1. Wiersbe, *Real Worship,* 149.

2. John Garmo, *Lifestyle Worship* (Nashville: Thomas Nelson Publishers, 1993), 18.

3. David Peterson, *Engaging With God,* 149.

4. Paul Lee Tan, *Encyclopedia of 7,700 Illustrations: Signs of the Times* (Rockville, MD: Assurance Publishers, 1979), 290.

5. D. E. Hiebert, "Satan," in *The Zondervan Pictorial Encyclopedia of the Bible,* Vol.5, 284.

6. Wiersbe, *Real Worship,* 147.

7. See John 1:17; Romans 3:24; 4:16; 5:2; 5:15; 5:17; 5:20-21; 6:14; 11:6; 1 Corinthians 1:4; Ephesians 1:6-7; 2:5; 2:7-8; 3:2; 4:7; 2 Timothy 1:9; Titus 2:11; 3:7; Hebrews 2:9.

8. Wiersbe, *Real Worship,* 147.

9. Wiersbe, *The Bible Exposition Commentary,* Vol. 1, 88.

10. G. E. Farley, "Circumcision," in *The Zondervan Pictorial Encyclopedia of the Bible,* Vol.1, 867.

11. Robert E. Webber, *Worship Old and New: A Biblical, Historical, and Practical Introduction Revised Edition* (Grand Rapids: Zondervan Publishing House, 1994), 106.

12. Robert E. Webber, *Worship Old and New: A Biblical, Historical, and Practical Introduction Revised Edition,* 106.

13. C. I. Scofield, ed., *New Scofield Reference Bible* (New York: Oxford University Press, 1967), 1213.

14. Peterson, *Engaging With God,* 27.
15. Wiersbe, *Real Worship,* 154.
16. Zodhiates, *The Complete Word Study New Testament,* s.v. "Thanatos," 919.
17. Edward Mote, *The Solid Rock, The Baptist Hymnal,* 406.
18. Wiersbe, *Real Worship,* 16.
19. Zodhiates, *The Complete Word Study New Testament,* s.v. "Matheteuo," 933.
20. Peterson, *Engaging With God,* 110.
21. Zodhiates, *The Complete Word Study New Testament,* "Metamorphoo," 936.
22. Wiersbe, *Real Worship,* 35.
23. Zodhiates, *The Complete Word Study New Testament,* "Latreuo," 931.
24. Albert W. Palmer in *Paths to the Presence of God* quoted in Thomas S. Kepler, comp., *The Fellowship of the Saints* (New York: Abingdon-Cokesbury, 1948), 680, cited in Wiersbe, *Real Worship,* 29.
25. Wiersbe, *Real Worship,* 38-39.

Chapter 9—The Invitation

1. Helen H. Lemmel, *Turn Your Eyes Upon Jesus* (Singspiration Music, 1922), in *The Baptist Hymnal,* 320.
2. This train of thought was inspired by a paragraph in, Judson Cornwall, *Elements of Worship* (South Plainfield: Bridge Publishing, Inc., 1985), 53.

Sources Consulted

Blanchard, John. *Gathered Gold*. Welwyn: Evangelical Press, 1984.

Bridges, Jerry. *The Pursuit of Holiness*. Colorado Springs: NavPress, 1978.

Cornwall, Judson. *Elements of Worship*. Plainfield: Bridge Publishing, 1985.

Giacumakis, G. "Desert." In *The Zondervan Pictorial Encyclopedia of the Bible*, edited by Merrill C. Tenney and Steve Barabas. Grand Rapids: Zondervan, 1976.

DeHaan, M. R. and Henry G. Bosch. *Bread for Each Day*. Grand Rapids: Zondervan, 1962.

Draper, James. *More Than a Song*. Chicago: Moody Monthly, 1970.

Forbis, Wesley L., editor. *The Baptist Hymnal*. Nashville: Convention Press, 1991.

Garmo, John. *Lifestyle Worship*. Nashville: Thomas Nelson Publishers, 1993.

Hayford, Jack. *Worship His Majesty*. Dallas: Word Publishing, 1987.

Henry, Matthew. *Commentary on the Whole Bible*. Edited by Leslie F. Church. Grand Rapids: Zondervan Publishing Company, 1960.

Hester, Dennis J., ed. *The Vance Havner Quote Book*. Grand Rapids: Baker Book House, 1986.

Hyles, Jack. "The Real Need of Evangelistic Music." In *How to Build an Evangelistic Music Program*, by Lindsey Terry, 19-20. Nashville: Thomas Nelson Publishers, 1974.

Knight, Walter B. *Knight's Master Book of New Illustrations*. Grand Rapids: William B. Eerdmans Publishing Co., 1956.

Kock, Sally. Cited in "Quotable Quotes," *Reader's Digest*, January 1994, 119.

Lee, Robert G. *Latest of Lee*. Jefferson City: Le Roi Publishers, 1973.

The Lockman Foundation. *The Amplified Bible*. Grand Rapids: Zondervan Publishing House, 1965.

Mathena, Harold. Telephone interview by Gary Mathena. 1 June 1994, Bethany, Oklahoma.

Mead, Frank S. *12,000 Religious Quotations*. Grand Rapids: Baker Book House, 1989.

Moen, Don, Jack W. Hayford, Tom Hartley, Tom Fettke, Camp Kirkland. *God With Us*. Mobile: Integrity Music, Inc., 1993.

MacRae, A. A. "Prophets and Prophecy." In *The Zondervan Pictorial Encyclopedia of the Bible*, edited by Merrill C. Tenney and Steven Barabas. Grand Rapids: Zondervan, 1976.

McMinn, Don. *A Heart Aflame!* Oklahoma City: NCM Press, 1993.

Patterson, Ben. *The Grand Essentials*. Waco: Word Books, 1987.

Peterson, David. *Engaging With God—A Biblical Theology of Worship*. Grand Rapids: William B. Eerdmans Publishing Co., 1992.

Sanders, J. Oswald. *Spiritual Leadership*. Chicago: Moody Press, 1967.

Spence, H. D. M. and Joseph S. Exell, eds. *The Pulpit Commentary*. Vol. 15, *Matthew* and Vol. 16, *Mark*. Grand Rapids: William B. Eerdmans Publishing, 1950.

Spradlin, Roger. *Imitating the Incarnation*. Sermon preached at Valley Baptist Church, 7 August 1994.

Tan, Paul Lee. *Encyclopedia of 7,700 Illustrations: Signs of the Times*. Rockville, MD: Assurance Publishers, 1979.

Tenney, Merrill C. *Handy Dictionary of the Bible*. Grand Rapids: Zondervan, 1965.

Tenney, Merrill C. and Steven Barabas, eds. *The Zondervan Pictorial Encyclopedia of the Bible*. Grand Rapids: Zondervan, 1976.

Tozer, A. W. *Whatever Happened to Worship?* Camp Hill: Christian Publication, 1985.

Vine, W. E. *The Expanded Vine's Expository Dictionary of New Testament Words*. Edited by John R. Kohlenberger. Minneapolis: Bethany House, 1984.

Webber, Robert E. "Preparations for Becoming a Worship Leader." *Worship Leader Magazine*, February/ March 1992, 10.

_____. *Worship Is a Verb*. Nashville: Abbott Martyn, 1992.

_____. *Worship Old and New*. Grand Rapids: Zondervan Publishing House, 1982.

_____. *Worship Old and New*. Rev. Ed. Grand Rapids: Zondervan Publishing House, 1994.

Webster's Seventh New Collegiate Dictionary, 1965 ed.

White, James F. *Introduction to Christian Worship*. Nashville: Abingdon Press, 1993.

Wiersbe, Warren W. *The Bible Exposition Commentary*. Vol. 1. Wheaton: Victor Books, 1989.

_____. *Real Worship It Will Transform Your Life*. Nashville: Thomas Nelson Publishers, 1986

Williams, Donald L. *The Israelite Cult and Christian Worship*. Edited by James M. Efird in *The Use of the Old Testament in the New and Other Essays: Studies in Honor of William Franklin Stinespring*. Durham, N. C.: Duke University Press, 1972. Quoted in *The Complete Library of Christian Worship*. Robert E. Webber, ed. Vol. 1, *The Biblical Foundations of Christian Worship*, 85. Nashville: Abbott Martyn, 1993.

Willmington, Harold L. *Willmington's Guide to the Bible*. Wheaton: Tyndale House, 1984.

Zodhiates, Spiros, ed. *The Complete Word Study New Testament*. Chattanooga: AMG Publishers, 1991.

Recommended Reading

Chapter 1—One Thing Needful

Allen, Ronald B. *And I Will Praise Him: A Guide to Personal Worship in the Psalms*. Grand Rapids: Kregal Academic & Professional, 1999. 264 pp.

Brown, Robert K. and Mark R. Norton. *The One Year Book of Hymns*. Wheaton: Tyndale House Publishers, Inc., 1995. 395 pp.

Packer, J. I. *Knowing God*. Downers Grove: InterVarsity Press, 1993. 286 pp.

Parks, Marty. *Quiet Moments for Worship Leaders: Scriptures, Meditations, and Prayers*. Kansas City: Beacon Hill Press of Kansas City, 2008. 160 pp.

Piper, John. *Desiring God, Revised Edition: Meditations of a Christian Hedonist*. Colorado Springs: Multnomah Publishing Group, 2011. 368 pp.

_____. *A Hunger for God: Desiring God Through Fasting and Prayer*. Wheaton: Crossway, 2013. 208 pp.

Wyrtzen, Don. *A Musician Looks at the Psalms: 365 Daily Meditations*. Nashville, B&H Books, 2004. 416 pp.

Chapter 2—Worship's Purpose: Introduction to Worship

Segler, Franklin M. *Christian Worship: It's Theology and Practice*. Nashville: B&H Academic, 2006. 336 pp.

Tozer, A. W. *Whatever Happened to Worship?: A Call to True Worship*. Chicago: Moody Publishers, 2012. 152 pp.

Webber, Robert E. *Worship Is a Verb: Celebrating God's Mighty Deeds of Salvation*. Peabody: Hendrickson Publishers, Inc., 2004. 225 pp.

Wiersbe, Warren. *Real Worship: Playground, Battleground, or Holy Ground?*. Grand Rapids: Baker Books, 2000. 224 pp.

Whaley, Vernon M. *Called to Worship: The Biblical Foundations of Our Response to God's Call*. Nashville: Thomas Nelson. Inc., 2009. 384 pp.

White, James F. *Introduction to Christian Worship*. Nashville: Abingdon Press, 2001. 326 pp.

Wright, N. T. *For All God's Worth: True Worship and the Calling of the Church*. Grand Rapids: Wm. B. Eerdmans, 2014. 140 pp.

Chapter 3—Worship's Procedure: Theology of Worship

Dawn, Marva J. *Reaching Out without Dumbing Down: A Theology of Worship for This Urgent Time*. Grand Rapids: Wm. B. Eerdmans Publishing Co., 1995. 316 pp.

_____. *A Royal "Waste" of Time: The Splendor of Worshiping God and Being Church for the World*. Grand Rapids: Wm. B. Eerdmans Publishing Co., 1999. 377 pp.

Due, Noel. *Created for Worship: From Genesis to Revelation to You*. Geanies House: Mentor, 2005. 320 pp.

Man, Ron. *Proclamation and Praise: Hebrews 2:12 and the Christology of Worship*. Eugene: Wipf & Stock Publishers, 2007. 105 pp.

Martin, Ralph P. *The Worship of God: Some Theological, Pastoral, and Practical Reflections*. Grand Rapids: William B. Eerdmans Publishing Company, 1982. 252 pp.

Old, Hughes Oliphant. *Themes and Variations for a Christian Doxology: Some Thoughts on the Theology of Worship*. Grand Rapids: William B. Eerdmans Publishing Company, 1992. 160 pp.

Peterson, David. *Engaging With God: A Biblical Theology of Worship*. Downers Grove: IVP Academic, 2002. 317 pp.

Ross, Allen P. *Recalling the Hope of Glory: Biblical Worship from the Garden to the New Creation*. Grand Rapids: Kregal Publications, 2006. 592 pp.

Chapter 4—Worship's Past: History of Worship

Borchert, Gerald L. *Worship in the New Testament: Divine Mystery and Human Response*. St. Louis: Chalice Press, 2008. 272 pp.

Banks, Robert. *Going to Church in the First Century*. Jacksonville: Seedsower Christian Publishing, 1990. 48 pp.

Bradshaw, Paul F. *The Search for the Origins of Christian Worship*. New York: Oxford University Press, 2002. 256 pp.

Hill, Andrew E. *Enter His Courts with Praise!: Old Testament Worship for the New Testament Church*. Grand Rapids: Baker Books, 1997. 384 pp.

Martin, Ralph P. *Worship in the Early Church*. Grand Rapids: William B. Eerdmans Publishing Company, 1975. 144 pp.

Old, Hughes Oliphant. *Worship, Revised and Expanded Edition: Reformed according to Scripture*. Louisville: Westminster/John Knox Press, 2002. 208 pp.

Towns, Elmer L. and Vernon M. Whaley. *Worship Through the Ages: How the Great Awakenings Shape Evangelical Worship*. Nashville: B&H Publishing Group, 2012. 416 pp.

Webber, Robert E. *Worship Old and New*. Grand Rapids: Zondervan Corporation, 1994. 288 pp.

White, James F. *A Brief History of Christian Worship*. Nashville: Abingdon Press, 1993. 192 pp.

_____. *Protestant Worship: Traditions in Transition*. Louisville: Westminster/John Knox Press, 1989. 256 pp.

Chapter 5—Worship's Pattern: Tabernacle Worship

Barber, Wayne, Eddie Rasnake, and Richard Shepherd. *Life Principles for Worship from the Tabernacle*. Chattanooga: AMG Publishers, 2001. 208 pp.

DeHaan, M. R. *The Tabernacle*. Grand Rapids: Zondervan Publishing House, 1979. 192 pp.

Olford, Stephen F. *The Tabernacle: Camping with God*. Grand Rapids: Kregel Academic & Professional, 2004. 160 pp.

Simpson, A. B. *Christ in the Tabernacle: An Old Testament Portrayal of the Christ of the New Testament*. Chicago: Moody Publishers, 2009. 98 pp.

Soltau, Henry W. *The Tabernacle, the Priesthood, and the Offerings*. Grand Rapids: Kregel Publications, 1994. 492 pp.

_____. *The Holy Vessels and Furniture of the Tabernacle*. Grand Rapids: Kregel Publications, 1971. 152 pp.

Chapter 6—Worship's Power: Praise and Worship

Best, Harold M. *Music Through the Eyes of Faith*. San Francisco: HarperOne, 1993. 225 pp.

_____. *Unceasing Worship: Biblical Perspectives on Worship and the Arts*. Downers Grove: InterVarsity Press, 2003. 226 pp.

Law, Terry. *The Power of Praise and Worship*. Shippensburg: Destiny Image Publishers, 2008. 366 pp.

Liesch, Barry. *The New Worship: Straight Talk on Music and the Church*. Grand Rapids: Baker Books 2001. 272 pp.

Morgan, Robert J. *Then Sings My Soul: 150 of the World's Greatest Hymn Stories*. Nashville: Thomas Nelson Publishers, 2003. 308 pp.

_____. *Then Sings My Soul, Book 2: 150 of the World's Greatest Hymn Stories*. Nashville: Thomas Nelson Publishers, 2004. 320 pp.

_____. *Then Sings My Soul, Book 3: The Story of Our Songs; Drawing Strength from the Great Hymns of Our Faith*. Nashville: Thomas Nelson Publishers, 2012. 320 pp.

Williamson, Dave. *God's Singers: A Guidebook for the Worship Leading Choir in the 21ˢᵗ Century*. Nashville: in:ciite media, 2010. 324 pp.

Chapter 7—Worship's Practice: The Heart of the Worship Leader

Boswell, Matt. *Doxology & Theology: How the Gospel Forms the Worship Leader*. Nashville: B&H Publishing Group, 2013. 256 pp.

Kauflin, Bob. *Worship Matters: Leading Others to Encounter the Greatness of God*. Wheaton: Crossway Books, 2008. 304 pp.

Kraeuter, Tom. *Keys to Becoming an Effective Worship Leader*. Lynnwood: Emerald Books, 2011. 144 pp.

Miller, Stephen. *Worship Leaders, We Are Not Rock Stars*. Chicago: Moody Publishers, 2013. 128 pp.

Navaro, Kevin J. *The Complete Worship Leader*. Grand Rapids: Baker Books, 2001. 208 pp.

Noland, Rory. *The Heart of the Artist: A Character-Building Guide for You and Your Ministry Team*. Grand Rapids: Zondervan, 1999. 352 pp.

_____. *The Worshiping Artist: Equipping You and Your Ministry Team to Lead Others in Worship*. Grand Rapids: Zondervan, 2007. 256 pp.

Park, Andy. *To Know You More: Cultivating the Heart of the Worship Leader*. Downers Grove: IVP Books, 2004. 272 pp.

Chapter 8—Worship's Priority: Lifestyle Worship

Adams, David V. *Lifestyle Worship: The Worship God Intended Then and Now*. Eugene: Wipf & Stock Publishers, 2010. 154 pp.

Edwards, David M. *Worship 365: The Power of a Worshipping Life*. Nashville: Broadman & Holman Publishers, 2006. 208 pp.

Harland, Mike and Stan Moser. *Seven Words of Worship: The Key to a Lifetime of Experiencing God*. Nashville: B&H Publishing Group, 2008. 256 pp.

MacArthur, John. *The Ultimate Priority*. Chicago: Moody Publishers, 2012. 224 pp.

Redman, Matt. *The Heart of Worship Files*. Grand Rapids: Bethany House Publishers, 2010. 208 pp.

_____. *The Unquenchable Worshipper: Coming back to the Heart of Worship*. Grand Rapids: Bethany House, 2001. 128 pp.

CPSIA information can be obtained
at www.ICGtesting.com
Printed in the USA
JSHW021704280522
26342JS00003B/13